INVISIBLE
LANDMINES

A GUIDE TO RECOVERING FREEDOM, PEACE, AND JOY

JOHNNY HENDERSON

BALBOA.
PRESS

A DIVISION OF HAY HOUSE

Scripture taken from the King James Version of the Bible.

Balboa Press books may be ordered through booksellers or by contacting:

Balboa Press
A Division of Hay House
1663 Liberty Drive
Bloomington, IN 47403
www.balboapress.com
1 (877) 407-4847

Print information available on the last page.

ISBN: 978-1-9822-2583-4 (sc)
ISBN: 978-1-9822-2584-1 (e)

Balboa Press rev. date: 07/26/2019

CONTENTS

DEDICATIONS

MOM

I honestly don't know where I would be without my mom. She did a great job raising me as a single mother. It was difficult for her at times. She always provided my basic needs and supported all my sporting activities. She did this all at the same time as working full time and pursuing her doctorate. Thanks Mom. It was especially difficult during my teenage years when I was getting into trouble and exercising my independence. Sorry, Mom.

Mom moved to California to restart her life after my 2nd year of college, and I stayed on the East Coast. She accomplished this life reboot, went on to remarry, and do very well for herself. Mom would visit us a few times a year and enjoyed the girls growing up. But it wasn't until my separation from my wife of 26 years that we became really great friends. She was there for me during this very turbulent time, and I really needed her to be. Again, I honestly don't know where I would be without her love, time and wisdom.

When it came time to review this guide with someone, it was my mom who helped me get this guide from inspiration to print. I am not sure I would have finished without her assistance. I certainly know that the messages inside of it wouldn't have been communicated as clearly. Thanks, Mom.

STEVE S.

Steve S. was a coach of mine. He was so humble. When I would thank him he would always give the credit to the God of His Understanding. Steve would simply say it was his duty to help others the way others helped him.

He would say if you are grateful for my help then help others in return. The following are some of his wise sayings.

"If you want to be a good brother, etc. then act like one."

"You can start your day over at any time."

"You can put the backpack down anytime you want."

"If you don't make it hard, then it won't be hard."

"The secret to happy living is wanting what you already have."

STEVE A.

Steve A. was a spiritual coach and a friend. He taught me to be gentle with myself. He was always there to help me. He allowed me to share my burdens and navigate many Landmines. Steve was there for me during the last years of my marriage and first year of my separation. These were dark and turbulent times. I am grateful for his help. Without it, I would feel regret. He helped me to understand that I did everything in my power to keep the marriage and family unit together. It is because of his help that I am able to move more freely towards the future with more peace than I otherwise would have.

TOM V.

Tom V. is a mentor and friend of mine. We met at our old church. We quickly realized we had a lot in common. He was older and more like a father figure or big brother. We play golf together and have breakfast consistently. He helps me navigate Landmines in my life, when I choose to reach out and ask for help. He helped me so much during my marital separation and divorce. He is my main "go to guy" when I am not in a good place. He helps me avoid a lot of Invisible Landmines and suffering.

PAIGE AND ABBY

My life would be incomplete without my two girls, Paige and Abby. I thank God for experiencing the gift of both of you. You are the greatest joy of my life. I am very proud of who you have become and will continue to be. Remember my theme song for you, "Forever Young." I pray you will always be willing to Embrace the WE.

INTRODUCTION

The purpose of this guide is to bring awareness and solutions to those who suffer, especially those with depression or addictions. Pain is inevitable, but suffering is optional. It is through liberation from my own suffering from depression and alcoholism that I desire to share some of my experiences with you. It is my mission to bring you good news that you don't have to suffer, and that you have a choice in the matter. Those with addictions don't have to suffer, but they will if they don't learn new skills and embrace the support of others and their God. **You can have freedom, peace, and joy regardless of your situation or circumstances.**

Invisible Landmines are obstacles in our path that keep us from ultimate freedom, peace, and joy. Many Landmines are invisible to us and lie within us. We are not aware of them until we "step on them" and hurt ourselves and those around us. We feel pain and can cause pain in others. Suffering follows if we don't have the proper Landmine Navigation skills to eliminate the pain. Pain will occur in life, but our reaction to the pain determines if we suffer or how long we will suffer.

To be successful in avoiding suffering, we need to become aware of these Landmines. Once we are aware of them, we can apply specific principles and solutions to accomplish our ultimate goal:

FREEDOM, PEACE, AND JOY

We accomplish this by living in the NOW, doing NO HARM to ourselves and others, and practicing Self-Care. If we do these things, we have an opportunity to celebrate the day in joy!

My solution to life's Invisible Landmines is a spiritual solution. When we recover our relationship with the God of Our Understanding, we recover our freedom, peace, and joy! Therefore, we will be spiritually focused in this guide.

It is from living in and out of the darkness for many years that this guide manifested. After I was freed from the darkness in 2001, I found peace and joy again. However, the darkness can reappear at any point if I am unaware of it, or I allow The Enemy's lies to dominate my thinking and actions. I don't want to give the impression that waking up spiritually is a one-time event. Yes, there is the first time awakening, and it is magical and beautiful. However, there is an on-going, daily event of Enemy Combat. It is a daily choice to practice Self-Care and Embrace the WE, the primary solution.

This is also the guide from which I operate my daily life and coach my clients. The guide is meant to bring awareness of hidden problems that we all face on our journey. I know that freedom, peace, and joy are available to all who seek them. I sincerely hope this guide helps you (or someone you know) and motivates you to end your suffering.

The following are my views out of my personal experience. They are only my views. I have tried my hardest to keep things as simple as possible. Simplicity works. If you find some things too simple, then I have accomplished my goal. It is from this point of view that I don't consider myself an expert on anything. However, inside this guide, I am an expert on my own experience; and I feel it is my responsibility to share it with you. I do have seventeen years of sobriety under my belt and have coached over 100 people on their path to recovery. I know that these ideas work. So I strongly suggest that you take what works for you and leave the rest. **I also strongly advise that you set aside any prejudice you might have towards the God subject because the solutions inside the guide have nothing to do with religion. The solutions deal with spirituality.** However, you and only you determine what you believe and what works best for you. Don't allow anyone to tell you otherwise! Please choose your own source of power.

Learning how to grow into an image of light or to become enlightened seems to be what this journey is all about. Understanding this need for enlightenment and utilizing the Core Principles are critical to our transformation.

This guide wouldn't be needed if our society and its young people would be happier. It appears to me that there is more suffering now than at any other time in my lifetime. Why is it a common occurrence for our teenagers to know a friend who has considered, attempted or succeeded at suicide? Collectively as a whole, these young people are simply not as happy as they should be or can be. Again, that is the purpose of this guide. My mission is to bring The Solution to the problem into awareness through my personal experience.

I have added song and Bible quotes that reinforce the important points in this guide. I hope you listen to the songs and read the Bible quotes. They will allow the spirit in them to lead you to joyful daily living! We are surrounded by The Spirit all the time, and I promise you will experience your own inspiration if you are seeking it.

HOW WE GOT HERE

God created the world. He created us for a relationship with Him and others. We were given everything we need for our freedom, peace, and joy. He is the Father; we are the children. That makes other human beings our brothers and sisters. In this world view, we are all connected spiritually. I see us as spiritual beings having a human experience. When I first heard of this, it was a new idea for me. When I understood this concept, things made sense. This was the key that unlocked the door to my spiritual progress. When I treated my problems spiritually first, the other aspects of my life followed. So the purpose of this guide is spiritual in nature and meant to be transformational.

It is important at this point to understand that it doesn't matter if you are an Atheist, Agnostic, Christian, Buddhist, Hindu, Jesuit or Muslim. We are talking about a source of power that will help us. Please choose your own concept of this higher power. Some call this power God, Father, Creator, Spirit of the Universe, Source, or Force. It doesn't matter to me what you call it because it is yours to define as you wish.

This brings us to the human condition. Some call this condition a disease. I know for sure that it most certainly causes "dis-ease." Most of us can agree that the human today could be happier. We don't experience the freedom, peace, and joy that God designed. Why do 25% of ninth graders surveyed in Charlotte, North Carolina admit to cutting themselves? Why is it that 33% of our adult community takes antidepressants? Why do we have an opiate/heroin crisis? Why do we have school shootings? Lastly, why is it common for our teens to have thoughts of suicide, have known someone who has thought about it, or have acted on suicidal thoughts?

I believe we are suffering from an Enemy force. This Enemy is real and powerful, and its main purpose is to accuse and deceive us. The Enemy's main lie begins with us believing we are separate from our Creator. I call any of The Enemy's lies, Invisible Landmines. When we believe The Enemy's lies, it puts us in a position of pain and possible suffering. One of The Enemy's lies tells us "We don't really have a problem." "That we are in control of our destiny, and we can go it alone." When we believe an Enemy lie, pain ensues. When we go it alone with our pain, we suffer. "Embracing the WE" is what I call the primary solution to the problem of going it alone. It is inside the WE that we find the spiritual solution that can solve any problem we have. (The Enemy, Invisible Landmines, and Embracing the WE are concepts described in Chapter 2.)

Without this spiritual solution of Embracing the WE, we will seek comfortable alternative solutions. Some of these alternative solutions may not be healthy, like overeating, undereating, drinking alcohol or taking drugs, gaming, pornography, gambling, dependence on others, overworking, over-exercising, binge watching, or worshiping money and success. You can fill in your own substitute solution as there are plenty of ways we attempt to treat ourselves when we don't feel good. If we don't treat ourselves spiritually, we will treat ourselves artificially. Furthermore, how much is enough? Is there ever enough? These artificial substitutions are temporary. If a treatment is unhealthy and habitual, it can lead to an addiction creating a secondary and bigger problem. We may think, "If I had a bigger house I would be happy." "If I had a prettier girlfriend I would be happy." "If I lost 20 pounds I would be happy." These thoughts might be true, but they are temporary, and are another example of The Enemy's lies (Invisible Landmines). What happens when we actually get what we seek? Are we happier? Yes, temporarily. What's next? An even bigger house? An even prettier girl friend? Lose another 20 pounds or plastic surgery? Do you get the point? When is there enough? Where does it end?

When we don't get the big house or when we lose the big house, what happens? Enter The Enemy and his biggest lie of all: "I am not happy. I am not going to be happy. I see no hope. There is no hope for the future.

Why should I keep living?" The real solution is one that is not temporary. It is a relationship with God and others that I call "Embracing the WE."

The purpose of this guide is to bring Awareness, appropriate tools, and effective Landmine Navigation skills. The ultimate goal of this guide is to liberate those who suffer in order to achieve freedom, peace and joy in the NOW. We accomplish this goal by developing Landmine Navigation skills in order to DO NO HARM to ourselves and others. The end result after practicing and developing these skills is love and compassion for ourselves and others. This is a "Life, I love you" kind of joyful experience.

"God created man in his own image; in the image of God he created him; male and female he created them." Genesis 1:27

CHAPTER 2

THREE MAJOR CONCEPTS

In this guide, we will focus on three important concepts that are the basis for my philosophy and programs. To avoid any confusion, this terminology will be explained up front as it will be utilized throughout the guide.

THE ENEMY AND ITS LIES

One of the reasons to not go it alone is because there is an Enemy who loves interacting with us when we are alone. We define The Enemy as any being or person who causes a disturbance with our peace. The Enemy is anyone who keeps me in darkness or prevents me from living in the present, the NOW. The Enemy lies to us. It deceives and accuses us. If we believe a lie that The Enemy tells us, then we are headed for trouble. We are prone to hurt ourselves and others if we act on a lie.

Often when The Enemy lies to us, we believe it. We believe it because we aren't aware of how persuasive and subtle The Enemy can be. The Enemy's job is to deceive us, accuse us, and to bring us out of the light and into the darkness. The Enemy tries to move us toward suffering and away from freedom, peace, and joy. The Enemy is real and powerful through its deceit. We will believe Its lies and accusations and suffer because of our inevitable freedom of choice.

4

The Enemy wants me in Hell. It wants me to hurt myself and others. It wants me to stay locked in the prison of myself where I am vulnerable to Its lies. It appears to me that deception is Its only power over us. The Enemy is real and can be called Satan or the Devil.

Buddha called the darkness suffering. The Christian church said we were broken. The ancient Toltecs called it Mitote. It is all the same thing. It is a dark horrible place where I don't want to be again. It doesn't work for me. The Enemy wants to get and keep me there.

The Enemy is also ME, my human ego, and my self-centered thinking. I believe we have two parts: a higher self and a lower self. The lower self is human and is a slave to our survival instincts. The higher self is our true self and our spiritual potential. It is our DNA of God. **I am the one who gets in my own way.** I am the one who is the slow learner. I am the one who allows others to hurt me and replays the pain causing suffering. I am the one who retaliates and causes more pain. So I am my own enemy.

It appears that The Enemy is complex, multi-faceted, and around us (or in us) all the time. It is real and powerful. The good news is The Enemy can be dealt with, and victory can happen. But if victory is going to happen, we must become aware of The Enemy and understand its purpose and goal of bringing us suffering.

"Settle down, it'll all be clear. Pay no attention to the demons they fill you with fear. Know that you are not alone." – "Home" Philip Philips

"Be sober, be vigilant; because your adversary the devil walks about like a roaring lion, seeking whom he may devour." 1 Peter 5:8

Here are some of The Enemy's lies. Don't let it deceive you!
#1 Lie: "Life is not worth living, and I am better off dead."

This is the most serious lie, and there was a time when I was believing it. There was a time when I wanted to die. I surely am thankful that I didn't take Action on this Enemy lie.

You may be thinking, "What's the point? My life doesn't matter anyway! No one will miss me! I will never get ahead! I will never be able to live with what I did."

You can survive the lies of The Enemy and move through life with freedom, peace, and joy. However, if you believe this lie long enough, then you might make the ultimate sacrifice. I beg you to not dance with The Enemy very long by yourself. It is dangerous to do so. There are just too many stories of those taking their own lives because they simply believed this most serious lie and lost hope. Chances are that they went it alone instead of Embracing the WE. Chances are they didn't have sufficient Enemy Combat Skills which are found in Chapter 6 and throughout this guide.

If you take one thing from this book, take this: Life is worth living and suffering can end if you Embrace the WE!!! I promise you this truth!!!!

#2 Lie: "We are separated from others and the God of Our Understanding."

This Illusion is all based on a lie that we are separated from our Creator and separated from each other. When we believe this lie, we suffer. The suffering continues if we go it alone. This Enemy lie is a problem and part of our human condition. The Enemy tells us that we are all alone and separated from our Creator, and/or we are separated from each other. When we believe that we are connected to each other and God we are less likely to harm ourselves or each other.

Buddha talked about the Illusion that we are in fact separate from God. All of our suffering traces back to this perception that we are separate. We then think of ourselves as independent or apart from our Creator or the Universe. We also think of ourselves separate from our fellow travelers. Jesus called the Creator of life his Father, and the people around him his Brothers and Sisters. Why? Because Jesus discovered the solution. He discovered that we were all connected. That we were in fact ONE. He experienced Heaven on earth. This truth set him free to see past The Enemy's lies. The biggest lie was that we were separate from God and others. He found the Spirit. He found the energy that connects us all. He found spirituality and in so doing he found himself and his true nature.

Since we think of ourselves as separate, we think about ourselves a lot. We think about ourselves most of the time. As soon as I think about myself I begin to desire something. As soon as I start to desire something, I move away from Heaven and start towards Hell but I may not know it. I believe

Heaven is NOW. I believe Hell is NOT. As soon as I desire something, it moves me into the future and out of the NOW. This future dream state is another lie. My mind tells me that if I only had _____, then I would be happy. What usually happens in this future dream state filled with desire? Fear usually follows. I start thinking that I won't receive it. I take Action to get it. What inevitably occurs is that I am on a collision course with a Landmine. We are tricked into believing we need something, when the reality is we already have everything we need.

"We belong to the light. We belong to the thunder. We belong together." – "We Belong" Pat Benatar

"Deep inside we're all the same." -- "Grand Illusion" STYX

Lie #3: "Life should not be painful."
For a long time I didn't understand why God allowed pain. I created an expectation that life would be pain-free. When pain came, I blamed others and God for it instead of taking ownership of what I did to cause it. Pain is necessary in order to learn, change and grow into our highest and best version of our self.

Lie #4: "Life is supposed to be fair"
Life is not fair. Why do I believe it when The Enemy tells me "Life is supposed to be fair?" Why do the rich get to be rich? Why does a welfare recipient get free money, and I have to work for everything I get? Why am I jealous of the rich man's money? Why am I jealous of the poor man's time? Why do I think life owes me anything in the first place?

Why do I get to see with my eyes when someone else is blind? Why do I get to walk today when someone else is in a wheelchair? Why did I get to experience a high level of golf as a kid? Why did I get to be employed inside the golf industry for most of my career? What a blessing that I have carved out a living inside a game. Why did I get to meet and marry a gal who is so much better then I deserve? Why is it that my wife and I received the blessing of kids when others can't have them? Why do others lose their children? One of the most positive people I know had 4 miscarriages. Oh, the pain that must have been! How is that fair? It's not. It's a lie to believe that life is fair.

So, the real question is not "Why doesn't life give me what I deserve," but rather, "What am I going to do about life when it doesn't give me what I think I deserve?" What choice am I going to make? Lemons or lemonade? Blame God for not being fair or thank Him/Her/It for the blessings that I have? When is the last time I actually counted my blessings or took an inventory for all of the wonderful things I have received?

I felt cheated by the early death of my father. He was 57 and had recently retired to Myrtle Beach, SC. He was living his dream after a hard life of working, raising families, and trying to do the right things. And bam! He had a massive heart attack on his anniversary. How could you allow that one, God? My dad was only 3 hours away from me instead of 12 hours back in Michigan. I was in the process of buying a boat for us to go fishing. Not fair, I thought. But then a few years later, I watched my mom deal with the aging of her dad. I watched my wife deal with her dad and aunt as they grew old and became immobile. It takes a great deal of time, money, and emotional strength to deal with end-of-life situations. Then there's the guilt you feel no matter what decisions you make. So, is it really unfair that Dad went fast, without cost or burden to family, and pain-free? Well, the cold hard reality is no one gets out alive. The real problem is my believing that life is supposed to be fair. What do I know? When reality hits me between the eyes, isn't it true that I should be grateful that I didn't get what I thought I wanted?

<u>Lie #5: "I am not good enough," "I don't have enough," or "I don't do enough."</u>

I suffered from The Enemy's internal voice for years. I still do listen from time to time when I don't realize that I am doing it. The Enemy tells me "I am not doing enough. If only I did more, I would be happy." That's a lie. "If only I had that BMW, then I would be happy." That's a lie. So many young girls look in the mirror and say. "If only I were thinner, I would be happy." That's a lie.

<u>Lie #6: "I, The Enemy, don't exist." This might be the biggest lie of all. If The Enemy doesn't exist then It has a free pass to deceive us at will. I must learn to recognize the voice of The Enemy and not believe Its lies.</u>

INVISIBLE LANDMINES

We have determined that The Enemy is real and lies to us. When we believe these lies, they become obstacles in our path to peace. These obstacles prevent us from living in the present moment, from living in the NOW. I call such an obstacle a "Landmine." Some Landmines are visible and some are invisible. A visible Landmine is one of which I am aware. An Invisible Landmine is one of which I am not aware and can be surprised. The good news is we have an opportunity to learn Landmine Navigation if we are aware of the Landmines because they are visible. So our primary goal with Landmines is to change each Invisible Landmine to a visible one by developing the skill of Awareness. That way we avoid "stepping on the Landmine" and feeling pain.

In addition to The Enemy's lies, there is another type of Invisible Landmine which is the expectations we create. We create expectations about others, God, and how life is supposed to go. When life doesn't occur like we planned it, we are hurt. We are disappointed. We are in pain. Ideally we shouldn't create any expectations in the first place. But we are humans, and we will create them. It is part of the reality of the human condition. We create them even though the result of the expectation is out of our control.

This is an example of an Invisible Landmine. One day, I was minding my own business driving down the road when a driver cut in front of me and then flipped me off. This pissed me off. However, it is a spiritual truth that when my peace is disturbed there is ALWAYS a part I played. This is true 100% of the time. So what was my part in this incident? What did I do wrong? I was just driving along before this selfish stranger decided to cut me off then flip me off. The answer is I EXPECTED him to not be a jerk and not act this way. I expected him to practice the Golden Rule. I expected him to DO NO HARM. **I am the one who created that expectation**. I am the one who created that Invisible Landmine. I am the one who allowed this guy to cause me pain. I am the one who allowed my pain. Although he caused the incident, it was my response which determined if I would get irritated or not. I was the one who could potentially let this event ruin my entire day and cause suffering if I chose to stay in the problem instead of embracing a solution and taking Action that worked for me.

Anytime we have a disturbance in our peace, we have encountered a Landmine. We need to navigate the Landmine if we desire peace because a Landmine will prevent us from obtaining our daily goal of experiencing freedom, peace, and joy. This guide is all about learning how to identify and navigate these Landmines so we can be free and have peace. Once we have freedom and peace, we have the opportunity for joy.

EMBRACING THE WE: THE SOLUTION

"Embracing the WE" is the primary defense against The Enemy. It is the solution to the problem of isolation and going it alone. Embracing the WE means that we ask for help and form a relationship with the Power above us, the Power within us, and the humans around us. These relationships are the foundation for successful living. The concept of The WE can be represented visually by a plus sign or a cross indicating its vertical and horizontal nature.

THE VERTICAL WE

The vertical line in the concept of The WE represents our connection or relationship with God, the Source of All, the God of My Understanding or the Power Greater than Myself. It can be the God of Heavens, the God Within, or the God that Surrounds Us All. It is your God to be defined anyway you see fit. But the relationship is vertical for our discussion purposes because the relationship is with a power greater than ourselves.

I am a child of God and that implies that I am an offspring of God. This means to me that I am created with the same stuff as God. This means that you are too. I like to think of it like this: God is a big beautiful sandy beach. When we look, it appears to be a beach and nothing else. But the beach is made up of trillions of tiny particles of sand. You and I are specks of sand. We are a part of the beach. We are not the beach, but we are a part of the beach. Therefore, a piece of God is in each one of us. This explains how we are connected to God and others spiritually.

I woke up in my hotel in Richmond, Virginia where I had traveled for work as a Regional Sales Manager selling golf operation software. I got a call from Deb, my stepmother. She told me my father had a heart attack that morning and had died. It was their wedding anniversary and he was only 57.

I jumped in my car and took off for Myrtle Beach where they lived. The car radio was on. I heard a pastor delivering a sermon. This was odd. I had been listening to music the night before. This pastor was delivering the message to these two young kids that God was promising them that their father was in heaven with him. I immediately started crying. I knew right then that I had experienced God. I knew right there that my Dad was ok, that he was in heaven and that there was a place we go after death. I delivered that story in the eulogy to my little brother and sister. I don't know if they or anyone else believed me, but it happened. I can't explain how it did. I only know it did. It was more evidence that God was real and cared about me. I knew it would all be ok now and in the future. This life is not all there is.

HORIZONTAL WE

The horizontal line in the concept of the WE is comprised of our relationship with our fellow humans, fellow spiritual travelers, brothers, sisters, friends, family and neighbors. The horizontal line allows God to work through others. I have found this is the primary way that God communicates with me. Perhaps you will find that too.

An example of the Horizontal WE is when I asked for my mother's help to collaborate on the writing of this guide because I was stuck on my own. When I sought help outside myself, that help could make my thoughts and words become more sensible to others. Unfortunately, one must experience enough pain and suffering from going it alone in order to become willing to ask for or accept help. As time goes on, we come to rely on the power of the WE based on tangible evidence that it works better than going it alone. WE can do what I can't do alone.

When we choose to ask for help it is wise to ask someone who has knowledge and specific personal experience on that topic. It is easier to ask for help from someone we know and trust. This is where a referral comes in. Sometimes the correct advisor is referred to us by someone we know and trust.

Another example of the Horizontal WE is burden sharing. I believe we were designed to share our burdens. When I share my burdens with another human being I feel better. When a burden is shared it loses its power. If I share my burden with someone, my burden is usually eliminated or at worse cut in half. I might need to share my burden again. If I share the burden again and it is also cut in half, then now it's only 25% consuming me. When the engine on my wife's car stopped working and she was a stay at home mom, money was tight. I was fearful that this $5000 new engine would really set us back, and it did. However, the fear was greater than the reality. I kept sharing with others, kept Embracing the WE, and the painful emotion of it went away. The fear that the world was going to end went away. However, the $5000 bill for a new engine remained. As I continued sharing with others to lighten my burdens, I moved from Hell to Heaven where freedom, peace, and joy exist. Sharing the burden is always an Action step away from the darkness and towards the light.

For many years, I was carrying huge burdens everywhere I went. It was like a backpack full of rocks. Two of the rocks were my parents' divorce and my grandmother's suicide. As with everything, I needed to be aware of the truthful fact that my way wasn't working, and I needed to do something different. Embracing the WE and making a choice to share my burdens was something different that worked.

I remember being at my older kid's soccer game and being disturbed by something. I was obsessing about it. I spent the entire first half of the game watching the game but didn't see a play. I was not there mentally. I was grinding away at a past anger. I couldn't get past it until I became aware that I was in a dark place and chose to take Action by calling a friend. Simply by sharing my burden with another human being I was free from The Enemy's grasp and able to be present for the second half of the game.

As humans, we need accountability and others' help to hold us accountable. Accountability is an obligation or willingness to accept responsibility. It is very difficult to hold ourselves accountable. It is challenging to change. It is far easier to change and grow into a better version of ourselves when we embrace the Horizontal WE. The caddy in golf embodies Embracing the Horizontal WE concept. Bones, Phil

Mickelson's caddy, knows the yardage, has every yard of turf mapped out, and knows his player better than himself. Phil and Bones talk through every shot together. They leave no stone unturned in order to become as committed to the decision as possible. Bones encourages Phil when needed and calms him down when the golfer's hot head appears. Sometimes Bones brings Phil back to the NOW, where peak performance is possible and where hope for perfection dwells. The caddy is a partner. He shares in the success and the failure. The caddy shares in the prize money too when playing with the big boys. The caddy serves. He rakes the trap, replaces the divot, reads the putt, cleans the clubs, and organizes his player's bag. The caddy is the light behind the scene and never gets the accolades. He is just serving the WE partnership. Normal golfers don't have a caddy. No wonder most of us aren't that successful. Caddies are also coaches. They can help the player make on the spot adjustments which happens all the time. My point is that going it alone does not work nearly as well as Embracing the WE. A great example of a caddy can be found in the book and movie entitled, "The Legend of Baggar Vance."

The greatest benefit of Embracing the WE is not suffering by going it alone. We can benefit from Embracing the Vertical or Horizontal WE independently. Either WE is designed to end suffering. However, the combination of the two is where synergistic power dwells. This solution will free us from The Enemy's darkness and move us into the light where we can enjoy Heaven on earth and know peace and joy. On this journey as humans with our human condition, it is impossible to navigate Landmines without suffering if we go it alone. So, Embracing the WE is necessary in order to not suffer and have freedom, peace, and joy!

Embracing the WE is a skill that can be learned, when one is willing. It is a learned skill to ask for help. So we ask for help from either God and/or others. Embracing the WE is like building our house on a rock so it will stand up to adversity. My relationship with God and others is that rock. The wind will blow. The rain will come down. Pain will happen. It is inevitable. So, we build our house on a rock called Embracing the WE so we don't have to suffer when the pain comes. It works if we chose to not go it alone and Embrace the WE.

"When 2 or more are gathered, I will be there." Matthew 18:20

CHAPTER 3

TOP 10 CORE PRINCIPLES

The following 10 Core Principles are critically important for our success in Landmine Navigation and recovering our freedom, peace, and joy. They have changed my life for the better, and I hope they will do the same for you.

PRINCIPLE #1: RESPONSIBILITY FOR MY OWN FREEDOM, PEACE, AND JOY

We are responsible for our own freedom, peace, and joy. No one else is to blame. When we understand this core principle we can make progress. Many of us stay stuck in the past when others hurt us because we blame them. We never look at ourselves. We don't take ownership of our own attitudes.

If I don't take care of myself, who will? I must take responsibility for myself. I need to own my mistakes. I need to own my successes. I need to be responsible for my own freedom and peace. I need to be responsible for my own Self-Care. I need to be responsible for decreasing the power of The Enemy and increasing the God Spirit within.

It is a spiritual truth that 100% of the time when our peace is disturbed, there is something we did to cause it. Most people blame others instead of looking at what we did to cause the hurt or anger. Others will harm us but it is our problem, not theirs. It is imperative that we always look for our part if we want to be free. It is our own side of the street that we want to be clean. We need to own our part that led to the disturbance in our peace.

This is a very difficult concept to grasp at first. How can it be that if my car got broken into last night I have a part in causing it? I didn't do anything to cause my car to be broken into but my reaction may cause my peace to be disturbed. If I let my peace be disturbed, then I become part of the cause. In this case, I believed an Enemy lie that my car wouldn't be broken into. I expected my car to not be broken into. I expected others to DO NO HARM. However, if I got angry or upset in response to The Enemy's lies then I have a part in causing my peace to be disturbed. We don't want to believe lies or have our peace disturbed. Understanding, believing, and practicing this skill of taking responsibility for my part in a disturbance will pay dividends in our quest for freedom, peace, and joy.

"No one is to blame" -- "No One is to Blame" Howard Jones

PRINCIPLE #2: W-H-O: WILLINGNESS, HONESTY, AND OPEN MINDEDNESS

Willingness, Honesty and Open Mindedness comprise the acronym W-H-O. All three characteristics are necessary for positive change to occur. Without them, we will not change in a way that leads to ultimate freedom, peace, and joy. I can't emphasize this enough. We must apply the principles of W-H-O, if we want to accomplish our goal and maximize our success.

WILLINGNESS

Positive change begins with willingness. Willingness is the key that unlocks the good stuff that awaits us behind the unknown door. After I have become aware that my way isn't working and I have chosen to change, I must ask myself the following questions:

Am I <u>willing</u> to accept the fact that The Enemy is real and extremely powerful?

Am I <u>willing</u> to accept that I might suffer needlessly if I try to combat The Enemy alone?

Am I <u>willing</u> to Embrace the WE and not go it alone?

Am I <u>willing</u> to ask others for help and to hear their personal experience and wisdom?

Am I <u>willing</u> to ask the GOD of My Understanding for help?

Am I <u>willing</u> to take Action on the things I can change?

Am I <u>willing</u> to accept the things I can't change?

Am I <u>willing</u> to open up my mind and throw away old ideas that don't work anymore?

Am I <u>willing</u> to be honest with myself?

Am I <u>willing</u> to be honest with others?

Awareness shows us the door but willingness unlocks it. It is my personal experience that willingness is necessary to have ultimate freedom, peace, and joy.

HONESTY

Honesty with one's self is required for positive spiritual transformation. We begin to be honest with ourselves by first being honest with others. I wasted so much of my precious life because I simply couldn't be honest with myself. I couldn't be honest with the fact that my way wasn't working. Some call this denial. Denial is powerful. The Enemy and Its lies are very, very powerful.

I caused harm in my relationships. A large portion of this harm was due to dishonesty. This dishonesty hurt the trust others had in me. Trust is the foundation of relationships. I needed to learn how to be honest with others. When I developed this skill in all my affairs, I received trust. When I received trust my relationships improved. So, honesty with one's self and others is critical.

OPEN MINDEDNESS

Having an open mind is simply allowing us to be flexible to accept new ideas. It was my own pre-conceived ideas that kept me in my self-constructed prison of suffering for so long. It was unnecessary. I knew my way wasn't working but I couldn't see another way. I had a closed mind. It's like refusing to eat lima beans before ever trying them.

My mind had slammed shut to the God idea. If God was real, why did he allow all this suffering in the world? Why would he take my best friend at the age of 22? Why? Why? Why? Never did I offer a thank you, by the way. I think most of us have asked similar why questions. This journey called life certainly has its share of sorrow but staying in that sorrow and suffering is a choice. It was my closed mind that kept me there. I pray that you will put aside your pre-conceived ideas about spirituality and open up to the good stuff that I promise awaits you in the light on the other side of darkness' door.

There was a time when I heard the word, "Jesus," I would cringe and avoid the conversation whenever and wherever possible. Somewhere along my path to Hell, running on my free will, I closed my mind to Christianity or Jesus or anything else related to the subject. I made a choice to have nothing to do with it. Perhaps, it was my best friend's death. Perhaps it was my grandmother's suicide. Perhaps, I judged Jesus as just another impossible to believe story. I beg you to not make the same judgement right now. Please try to have an open mind before making a choice to dismiss Spirituality. The choice is always YOURS! I now attend a Christian church where my girls are involved in youth group. God, Jesus, and I are in a good place. I have found pieces of wisdom in Christianity, Buddhism, Islam and Hinduism because I was willing to have an open mind and be honest with what I find.

Willingness is the key that unlocks light's door out of the darkness. If I am open minded enough to believe the light is there and honest enough to believe I am in the darkness, then am I willing to be open minded and honest enough to walk through the door?

PRINCIPLE #3: THE SERENITY PRAYER AND ITS APPLICATION

I have found the Serenity Prayer to be invaluable. It has saved me many times over. I experience freedom and have a chance of joy when I apply it. It works.

God grant me the serenity to accept the things I cannot change,
Courage to change the things I can,
And the wisdom to know the difference.

This prayer works whenever I become aware that I have a disturbance in my peace, desire to stop experiencing pain, and choose to apply it. I remind myself that I am only a step away from peace again and ask myself this question:

"Do I have any control over the disturbance?"

If the answer is "No," then Acceptance is my answer. If the answer is "Yes," then I have control over the disturbance and Action is my answer. It is just this simple.

ACCEPTANCE (THE FIRST A)

According to the first line of the Serenity Prayer, Acceptance is the answer to all my problems that I don't have any control over. Here is an example of choosing Acceptance when I found myself in a situation that I could not change or control. My friend had a new lawn care business, and I needed my yard done. It dawned on me that I might be able to work out a deal with him that would help both of us. I could get some exercise by helping him for a few hours; and in return, I would get my yard done. He liked my idea. Well, my first 5 hour day of aerating started and I realized he wanted it done a certain way. It was his business, so I understood it would be his way. However, after doing three people's yards his way, I realized I couldn't physically continue due to my strained rotator cuff. He understood but we certainly disagreed about how I was going to be compensated. I was upset because I tried to help out a friend, and he didn't see it that way. It was an Invisible Landmine that I expected to be able to honor my commitments, help him, and get my yard done in the process. It was an Invisible Landmine that I expected him to appreciate my intentions and still help me with my yard. Once the Landmines were painfully visible, I used Acceptance of a situation that I had no control over to get back to my peaceful state in the NOW where I had clarity of the situation. I accepted that his way was acceptable and chose to not let this incident carry over to hurt the relationship.

The second lesson about Acceptance is in the very first words in the Serenity Prayer, "God, grant me the serenity." The word "God" suggests that I need to Embrace the Vertical WE and ask for help. If I had the skill to accept things I can't change on my own, I wouldn't need God. I wouldn't need the vertical help. But I didn't have that skill years ago. Now after many years of developing the discipline of asking God for help, Acceptance is very natural. It just happens out of habit now. However, it is definitely a learned skill.

What about when there is a bigger disturbance in our peace? What happens when a personal goal or dream is lost? I have several lost dreams.

1) The loss of my original dream of being a high end private club golf pro.
2) The loss of a business.
3) The loss of a marriage/relationship of 26 years and loss of a happy and united family unit.
4) The loss of my best friend.
5) The loss of my father and grandmother
6) The loss of my children as they grow up and leave home
7) The loss of our family dog and faithful companion, Roxie

I know you have losses too. Please fill in blank with your own losses:

_____

_____

_____

_____

No matter whether the problem is small or big, the question is still the same. I ask myself, "Do I have any control over it?" If the answer is "No, nothing" then Acceptance is the answer. Accepting things I can't change is a simple concept but it is not easy to do. In fact, it is the single most difficult thing I have had to do. Or actually <u>not</u> do! If the answer is Acceptance, then there isn't any Action to take. Learning how to live life on life's terms is a learned skill. It works for me much better than <u>not</u>

accepting things. When I wasn't able to accept things which I couldn't control, I often became angry, resentful, and blocked off from the NOW. Learning to accept things is a much happier way to live life.

ACTION (THE SECOND A)

Action is the answer to all of my problems that I have control over. So when there is something that I can do to change a situation, then I need to take Action by grabbing a tool to navigate the Landmine.

But what if I am afraid to take the Action? Well, here comes The Serenity Prayer again. It suggests that we ask the Vertical We for courage to change the things we can. We can also ask for strength to take the Action.

What about "the wisdom to know the difference" from the Serenity Prayer? Where does this part come into play? Wisdom deals with the uncertainty of which path to take towards freedom, peace, and joy. It deals with which A to choose, Acceptance or Action. If I am not sure which A to choose, wisdom suggests I once again ask for God's help or the help of others to give me the wisdom to know.

PRINCIPLE #4: DETACHMENT FROM OUTCOMES

Detaching from outcomes is liberating. Do your best, and let the results rest. I can only control my actions. I can't control the results.

Somewhere along the line, I started believing a lie, a big lie. The lie was and is that if I got what I wanted then I would be happy. If only I got the desired results from the Universe and its inhabitants, then all would be well with me. This is a lie. This is an Invisible Landmine. I will be happy once my kid becomes a golfer. I will be happy when I have my own business. I will happy as soon as my wife changes. I will be happy once my business partners deliver on time. I will be happy as soon as my dog isn't sick anymore. I will be happy when my kid stops acting like a teenager. Get the picture? Can you see the trend? I am attaching my happiness to others. I am attaching my happiness to outcomes. I am placing my happiness in the hands of other imperfect human creatures who have enemies of their own.

However, it doesn't matter about the other people. My Invisible Landmine was my own expectation of happiness if I got the result I wanted. My belief was the lie. I would try my hardest to get the result. This moved me farther down the path to Hell. I did not have peace. The result wasn't being delivered. I was getting angry. I was becoming sad. I was trying harder and harder. This process inevitably caused some carnage with others in a round of demolition derby. The truth is I have enough. I am enough. I do enough.

I started my own company because I was convinced that would solve several problems. It did solve several problems, but several other problems replaced them. The new venture did not solve the big problem, which was my unhappiness. Only the temporary elimination of The Enemy itself can heal my discontent. Notice that The Enemy is only temporarily eliminated. The Bible warns me to watch out. Once The Enemy is temporarily removed, he will wait patiently until I am vulnerable again. He will come back with many friends to attack.

I was jammed up by a resentment at my wife for a number of years. The details aren't important but I didn't think that it was fair. I blamed her. This deep cut would be triggered by any number of tiny and insignificant things that didn't go my way, like opening a cupboard and stuff falling out or the salt shaker not being where it was supposed to be. I was in Hell. I was not free or at peace. What made this era of our relationship the worst was my actions. I was an angry man. Everyone could see that I was overreacting beyond what the perceived wrong of my wife should cause. I was totally blinded by this resentment. My oldest daughter said to me, "Dad, why are you always so angry?" It wasn't until my legacy of a Great Dad was in jeopardy that I woke up to the possibility that I was wrong. I needed to accept my wife as she was. Lord knows she had done a much better job of trying to live her life and let me live mine.

Surrendering is a concept of giving the outcomes to the God of Our Understanding. We are responsible for our thoughts and actions but not the results. God is responsible for the results. This is a liberating concept. I live by it and it works.

Life becomes a lot simpler when I don't have a way. What I mean by this is my only responsibility is to stay in the NOW and go do the next right thing. I am free from the results with this attitude. I am more at peace when I don't have a way. I am in a state of living in the NOW when I keep my head where my feet are and when I am fully surrendered to the will of God. It is then that I experience freedom and peace.

"Some people claim that there is a woman to blame. But I know, it's my own damn fault." -- "Margaritaville" by Jimmy Buffet

PRINCIPLE #5: LIVE AND LET LIVE

Live and Let Live means to focus on ourselves and what we have control over and to allow others to do the same. When we stay out of the business of others, we are letting them live. This core principle has everything to do with understanding the difference between what is and what is not my responsibility.

Boundaries are mental barriers we have established to protect ourselves. The boundaries are based on our experience of what works for us. I like to refer to these boundaries as Hula Hoops. A Hula Hoop is a small circular ring, and when I step inside it surrounds me. This visual concept is designed to encourage me to stay inside of my boundary and to keep others out of my territory. Don't I have enough problems of my own inside my own hula hoop? Why do I need to take on your problems and those of the world? So I try to stay focused on what is my business, stay inside my hula hoop, and do my best with what I can control.

Loved ones of addicts are commonly found crossing over boundaries. It is very tricky. Where is the line of loving, serving, and helping someone and not helping someone? Sometimes our version of helping is actually hurting. This is called "enabling." I can't control you or your business. It is not in my hula hoop!

Who doesn't care about what others think of us? We all do care, but this truly becomes dangerous if we give all of our power to others. We give others power if we let them determine our value, worth, or direction in life. We give others power if we allow them to judge us. When I am practicing this skill correctly and effectively, I really don't care what you think because I am a child of God and am loved. God loves me. There is nothing you or anyone else can say or do to change that. The real question is am I going to allow you to dictate power over me? No, thanks. I want to keep my power today; therefore, what others think about me is NONE of my business. It is outside my hula hoop and my mental barrier.

I like to be liked. Who doesn't? I like to please people. I like to help them. This Invisible Landmine occurs when I sacrifice what I want in order to make other people happy. The situation usually ends in neither one of the parties getting what he or she wants and in both parties being disappointed. If I want to give to you and be of service to you then I need to make that decision. It is my decision to make. Doing what we don't want to do it in order to be liked or accepted causes pain and resentment.

PRINCIPLE #6: ATTITUDE OF GRATITUDE

We are as happy as we are grateful. It is that simple. Life can be difficult, and we will lose some daily battles with The Enemy. When I can frequently remind myself of all the truly amazing blessings I have received, my perceived problems decrease. Gratitude works. However, like all of these principles, it takes practice to develop the skill to become a natural part of daily living. Becoming sincerely grateful is a process which begins with making a gratitude list of all the things for which we are grateful. We count our blessings. Most of us have lost our way in this area because we haven't struggled to eat or have a roof over our head. Somewhere along the line, we got a sense of entitlement, that life owed us something. We lost our sense of gratitude. We need to develop a daily discipline of an attitude of gratitude.

For example, some days we don't want to go to work or clean our room. There are things that we don't want to do. It's natural to have an attitude of I **got** to do this. When we have a proper Attitude of Gratitude where today is a gift, then everything inside the day is a gift. So I **get** to go to work, or I **get** to clean my room. We are attempting to attain a sincere attitude of: I **GET** to do this instead of I **GOT** to do it. If we develop this skill properly, we will be happier, and also we will be grounded with sincere appreciation for what we have.

"A thankful heart is a happy heart, that is why I say 'thank you' every day." Veggie Tales

"It's not having what you want, it's wanting what you've got. I'm gonna soak up the sun, gonna tell everyone to lighten up." – "Soak Up the Sun" Sheryl Crow

PRINCIPLE #7: COGNITIVE RESTRUCTURING

Cognitive restructuring is simply repairing our thinking, actions and reactions. Believing Enemy lies over a long period of time takes its toll on our freedom, peace, and joy. Negative thinking becomes a habit. Therefore, positive thinking can become a habit also. I tried to think my way into freedom, peace, and joy. I still do. There is a place for that thinking. In fact, it is a form of meditation called contemplation. However, I needed cognitive restructuring. Some call cognitive restructuring brain washing. Brain washing has a negative connotation. But my mind needed to be washed clean from its stinkin' thinkin'. My mind needed to be reborn. I needed a reboot. We accomplish this by acting our way into right thinking. It is by doing the next right thing that our positive thinking follows. Our actions are what matter. Our actions are what others judge us on. They say it usually takes at least one repetition of the new behavior for 30 consecutive days to form a habit. So making changes in our behavior takes time.

An example of acting your way to right thinking is this: I wanted to be a good brother. My brother and sister live far away, and we have a big age difference. We didn't grow up together. I would like to have a better relationship with them. But I hadn't picked up the phone to call them. This bothered me until I took the Action to call more frequently. If I want to be a better brother, I need to act like one. Just do it!

In order to be responsible we need to do things that we don't want to do. We cannot be free if we aren't responsible first. So we act our way into responsibility by doing what we don't want to do and by NOT doing what we want to do. Most people react when someone cuts them off in traffic. My first reaction is to retaliate. Restraining my first and natural reaction is an example of not doing what I want to do.

Over time and with practice this type of thinking becomes natural. My brain is restructured, and I feel better. Improved thinking follows improved actions.

PRINCIPLE #8: LIVING IN THE NOW

Living in the NOW is living in the present moment. **There is freedom, peace, and joy in living in the NOW.** Like all the tools in this guide, living in the NOW can be learned. When we are thinking about the past or the future, we are not in the NOW.

Two thieves, the future and the past, rob me of my time in the moment. My time should be in the here and NOW, the place true life exists. I have spent way too much time with these two Enemy thieves. They have stolen from me. The reality is I have allowed them to steal from me. I have allowed my freedom, peace, and joy to be diminished because of living in the future or the past instead of the NOW.

We need to spend some time planning for the future as we thoughtfully pick a career or consult experts to have enough money for retirement. At times, we need to contemplate. We should dream. But as soon as we start thinking about the future, we start playing God. We start creating Invisible Landmines, little creative expectations of how life is supposed to go. The dream is an Invisible Landmine buried in the ground until the day we realize that the dream isn't coming into reality. Pain occurs when I step on this Invisible Landmine. The point is not to spend so much time thinking about a dream. Instead we should take Action to achieve it.

Another thing happens when I get out in the future. Fear follows. We start fearing that we won't get the results of the plan. This fear is an Enemy lie. The results are up to God. We are only responsible for doing our best and letting the results rest. When we want the result very badly, then more fear is created. In my life, what usually happens is I try harder to accomplish the result which I have no control over. This generally results in pain to myself and others.

We all have our own chapter about the pains of the past. We all have loss: loss of loved ones, loss of dreams, loss of health or finances. The problem occurs when all our attention is on the past. We are having the present moment stolen from us. We are allowing The Enemy to win.

When yesterday's angers become today's angers then they are resentments. They are being resent causing us to replay the past. Resentments are spiritual poison. Very little peace or joy can occur until we break free from the past and its old hurts and resentments.

It is pleasant to replay old positive memories. But when most of our time in the past is spent on replaying old hurts and angers, this is neither freedom nor peace.

A great skill to develop is keeping our head where our feet are and living in the NOW. We can experience the maximum freedom, peace, and joy in the NOW. We take Action by doing the next right thing with a grateful heart. We develop this skill by practicing it over and over again until it becomes natural or second nature to us.

"The Power of NOW" Eckhart Tolle (1999)

PRINCIPLE #9: SPIRITUAL BEINGS HAVING A HUMAN EXPERIENCE

Several years ago, I was part of a discussion, and the topic was the God of Our Understanding. It dawned on me that I did not really understand the God thing that I was calling my Higher Power. I only knew that I had experienced hope when I previously had none. A great thing had happened to me, but I did not understand it. So I started seeking this God of My Understanding. During this seeking process, I started asking myself questions. To my amazement, I started getting the answers through other people when I didn't ask them the question. Which begs the question, "How can this be?" I started getting answers in songs, billboards, and books.

Over time, I discovered that we are all connected spiritually, and my understanding was complete. I thought I was a human being seeking a spiritual experience. What I found instead was that I was a spiritual being first, and was experiencing life in a human form.

We are spiritual beings having a human experience. We are all connected to a Power greater than ourselves and to each other. We are all part of the ONE. With this attitude, the world makes sense. When we understand and apply this concept we are in a much better position to DO NO HARM to each other and ourselves. When I hurt you I am in fact hurting me.

"We are spirits in the material world." – "Spirits in the Material World" Police

PRINCIPLE #10: PRACTICE: PROGRESS NOT PERFECTION

I have spent a lot of time seeking a solution to my problem of unhappiness. I have also spent a lot of time understanding the solution. I understand the solution so well that I have written a book about it and started a business. So, why is it that sometimes I still can't contain my anger? Why can't I control my sadness? Why can't I control my selfishness? Why can't I control my fears? Why can't I control my delusional thoughts? I have a head full of knowledge, but at times very little mastery. It is because I am suffering from the human condition where The Enemy lies to me. It is because I will never be perfect at Enemy Combat. It is because I will never be perfect at Landmine Navigation. Perfection is beyond our human capabilities and desiring it sets us up for disappointment. It is an Invisible Landmine.

Fortunately, making progress is what this journey is all about. One day at a time, we try to watch out for The Enemy's lies and navigate Landmines. We celebrate small steps of progress. We try not to replay our failures or dwell on our imperfections. We practice Cognitive Restructuring and use our tools appropriately.

We know perfection is not possible, but we can strive for it through progress. Repetition builds habits, good ones and bad ones. Some habits work for us, and others don't. I want to be free, at peace, and have so much joy in my life that I want to shout "Life, I love you." This is a goal but it is not a destination. We experience the goal but it only lasts until the next Invisible Landmine is stepped on. However, as we continue to practice these tools, we will make progress. We will be able to look back and realize that we haven't suffered in a long time. Yes, we will have pain, but we haven't suffered. This will happen because we have recovered by developing new skills. We did this by practicing, lots and lots of practicing.

Teaching imparts new information to a person. It is estimated that teaching makes up at most 5% of developing a new skill. However, practicing is 95% of the process. How do we know if we are practicing correctly? This is where Embracing the Horizontal WE and having a second set of eyes is extremely helpful. The maximum result comes from the combination of teaching, coaching, and practice. Coaching reiterates new information, provides reminders, and motivates us to continue to apply the new information. It is in the practice of applying this new information, with the help of God and others, that we develop a skill and move towards our goal of freedom, peace, and joy.

CHAPTER 4

NO PAIN, NO GAIN

PAIN AND SUFFERING

As a result of believing The Enemy's lies or reacting poorly to our own Landmines, we feel pain. If that pain continues we suffer. In this life, pain is inevitable, but suffering is optional. But why is pain inevitable?

It appears to me that in this life pain is necessary to allow for growth. Life is designed to cause us to grow or mature. A tree needs to be pruned from time to time in order to grow bigger and stronger. We are like a tree because we also need to be pruned from time to time. Sometimes we can only change and grow when an experience is painful enough to force us to change. We need to let go of the things that don't work for us in order to allow room for the things that do work for us. Things that work for us make us stronger and more capable. No pain, no gain.

To purify silver, the impurities need to be burned away. The silversmith holds the precious metal over the middle of the fire where it is the hottest until the impurities are burned away, and nothing is left but pure silver. Isn't refining what God does with us to purify us and change us?

God is allowing us to feel pain in order to grow into his image. We grow into light. We grow into love. We grow into strong members of His team in order to serve others.

"He will sit as a refiner and purifier of silver." Malachi 3:3

CHANGE: DOING SOMETHING DIFFERENT

It was through suffering that I became willing to change. I became willing to put my prejudice aside about spirituality and seek truth. It is through seeking the truth that I found MY TRUTH about the Universe, about the God of My Understanding, and the truth about me. Today, I am still seeking and trying to evolve into the best version of myself. Why? Because it works. I cherish my freedom, peace, and joy!

Change is usually not easy or comfortable. But if our way isn't working, then change is necessary. I have found that most humans are resistant to change. Why? I think it is because of fear, fear of the unknown. Also, there is uncertainty if the change will succeed. So, faith must play a part for the change to work. Of course, we can always decide after an honest effort of executing the change that it isn't working, and choose to make another change. Is that the worst thing that happens? Usually, as long as we don't lose hope and go it alone, changing again isn't a big deal. Almost every change I made in my life ended up being a positive one. Change led to personal growth and new experiences. When the pain or suffering is great enough, we are usually willing to change. We become willing to Embrace the WE, get help from others, and take Action toward our freedom!!!!! In my life, I just wanted to get out of the suffering and for the torment to end. However, often I had to have that gift of desperation in the darkness to become willing to Embrace the WE and step towards the light.

"Carry on my wayward son. There'll be peace when you are done. Lay your weary head to rest. Don't you cry no more." – "Carry On Wayward Son" Kansas

DENIAL AND INTERVENTION

Denial is the inability to recognize the reality of reality. What happens when I become aware of an Invisible Landmine but don't believe it is a problem? The answer will come in time. If it isn't a problem now then it may not cause pain. However, if it is a problem then it will cause pain and will need to be addressed to prevent the recurring pain called suffering. What happens when we are aware of the Landmine and it is causing us pain and suffering, but we refuse to deal with it? This is denial. Continued denial over time is Insanity. Insanity is not being able to differentiate the truth from falsehood. An example of insanity is doing the same thing over and over again, but expecting different results.

When denial is causing harm, an intervention is needed to bring awareness. This suggested intervention is a serious meeting where loved ones share their honest feelings about how the problem behavior affects them and the individual. Each person takes his turn sharing. An important ground rule is the individual in denial does not speak until everyone else has shared around the room.

The meeting might go something like this: "We love you, but you are killing yourself." "I don't want you to die. We have told you this before, but now we simply can't continue being a part of your current life the way you are choosing to live it." "You need to get help." (This is a great opportunity to bring in a coach to facilitate this process.)

"You're killing yourself if you don't believe it." -- "Fooling Yourself" (The Angry Young Man) Styx

HOPE

Our goal of freedom, peace, and joy is possible. It is my personal testimony to share with you that freedom from suffering is possible. It is a choice. We can be free. Life can and should be peaceful. Life can and should be joyful.

Life has peaks and valleys. It is always darkest before the dawn. When we are in the valley it appears that we will never out of the valley or get back to the peak. We need to remember that this too will pass, and we must NOT QUIT. We need to be persistent. My experience is that the valley always ends in time. However, the length of time it takes to pass is based on how willing we are to change, to apply the tools of this guide, and to develop vital Landmine Navigation skills like "Embracing the WE."

"Here comes the sun. Here comes the sun, and I say... It's all right." – "Here Comes the Sun" The Beatles

"Don't worry, about a thing. Cause every little thing, gonna be all right." – "Three Little Birds" Bob Marley

CHAPTER 5

THE BIG 3: DECISION MAKING FRAMEWORK FOR CHANGE

The Big 3 (Awareness, Does It Work or Does It Not, and Freedom of Choice) is the simple framework for making decisions to avoid pain and suffering. I have been using this three step framework with my clients and for myself for several years, and it works. It helps us see when change is needed.

STEP #1: AWARENESS

The end of suffering begins with Awareness. If I am unaware of an existing problem (or a problem behavior) then I don't know I need a solution. That's a big problem. So, the first step in the process of change is becoming consciously aware that I have a problem.

I was unaware of my depression problem for many years. Sometimes, even today as I am writing this, I fall victim to the belief that I don't have depression tendencies. It is tricky when I feel so good and when depression is in the past to remember that depression is not a one-time event. It is an ongoing occurrence that can pop up at any given time and dominate my freedom, peace, and joy. It is only through Awareness that I know I have a problem and that the problem hangs around silently in me, waiting for an opportunistic time to strike. It is through Awareness that I am able to understand my problem and accept it, one day at a time. It is only through Awareness that I am able to Embrace the Solution of the WE and remain in a state of Heaven, a state of freedom, peace, and joy.

We are not responsible for our own freedom, peace, and joy if we are unaware of a problem's existence. We are not responsible for what we do not know. How can I get in trouble as a 5 year old when I am eating glue if I have never been told not to eat glue? How can I know how to add 5 plus 5 if I have never been made aware of the process? That is why Awareness is the first step in the framework. However, once aware, I am responsible. We will make mistakes. This is how we learn. Hopefully, we can learn from our mistakes the first time and not repeat them over and over again, which is insanity.

I was unaware of my depression until I became aware that I was drinking to medicate it. Then I became aware that my drinking wasn't working for people around me. It was affecting me and others. My drinking caused a lot of pain and suffering.

The good news is that through suffering over time I became aware of my depression and problems with alcohol. Once aware, I Embraced the WE and found solutions that worked. I use these solutions daily. They work when I choose to apply them.

STEP # 2: DOES IT WORK OR DOES IT NOT?

If I am aware of a problem behavior, then the next step is to ask the question, "Does the problem behavior work for me or not? The behavior works for me if it is healthy, is in my best interest, or solves a problem. I thought my drinking was working for me when I was 16 because it made me feel good. However, in reality, my drinking was not working for me because it caused pain for my parents. It was not in my best interest either, but I couldn't see it. Behaviors are not working if they cause pain or have detrimental consequences.

Why would someone choose to continue suffering with a problem behavior? They wouldn't, unless they are unaware of the problem, or in denial. They are in The Enemy's trance. It takes an intervention to break through the lie and bring awareness. Unfortunately, it usually also takes pain and a lot of it. I stayed in my suffering because I kept repeating my same unproductive behaviors and expecting different results. I repeated the same mistakes over and over and over again, and I suffered for a long time as a result. The good news is that I am now aware of my insane tendency to repeat unproductive behaviors and know it does not work for me.

Some people may continue suffering because they may not know how to change their behavior. Some may have given up after previous failed attempts to change. Others may not have resilience and may give up before they really try. Some may not be persistent enough because it's hard for a person to keep trying. Often the suffering from the problem feels good in some way or serves some purpose. Frequently, the solution we choose, like alcohol abuse, is so powerful that it trumps all else. When we get to this point, we are addicted to a behavior that we actually think works for us, when it clearly is hurting us and others. We need help. We need to "Embrace the We."

If our way isn't working, what should we do? First, we should admit that our way isn't working. Second, we have to want to change.

We should ask ourselves:

1. Have I admitted that my way isn't working? __Yes __No
2. Am I willing to change? __ Yes __ No

If you have said "Yes" to both questions, then you are ready to move forward.

You will need two things. You need an understanding of the very real and powerful Enemy that you are facing. You will also need traveling companions on your journey. I was embarrassed to need or ask for help. So I didn't ask for help until my back was against the wall. I didn't realize that my journey could actually be easier when traveling with others. (This includes God.) I had been going it alone without any skills and suffering in the darkness against a powerful Enemy. No wonder I failed and suffered. It wasn't until my experienced friends and coach made me aware. Once I was aware that my way was problematic and not working and I was willing to change, then I moved closer to ending my suffering and finding freedom, peace, and joy.

STEP #3: FREEDOM OF CHOICE

The good news is we have choices! We can choose what works or what doesn't. We can choose not to suffer or continue suffering! It is our choice! When I finally became aware that I had a behavior problem that I couldn't solve and that wasn't working for me, then I had a choice to make. Did I want to end my suffering? I realized that pain was inevitable, but suffering was optional. I didn't want to suffer any more, and I made the choice to not suffer any more. Then I was open to choose a solution that would free me from my suffering and lead to peace and joy. Freedom of Choice led me to acquire skills I needed and relationships with other people who could help me. We are never able in this life to be completely free of pain. Loved ones die. Children get sick, and things don't go our way. People hurt us. Pain happens. However, we are able to cope and deal with painful situations better when we choose to learn new skills and have supportive people in our lives.

Sometimes when we are unhappy with our current life situation (our work, relationships, or where we live), we make decisions to change these circumstances instead of looking at our spiritual condition. We think that this choice will solve our problem. We think the grass will be greener. This is an example called a "geographic cure." If the underlying problem is our attitude or spiritual condition, a change in circumstance will not solve the problem. Wherever we go, the problem goes. When we improve our spiritual condition or the underlying problem, many times our living condition improves as well. Others through the Horizontal WE can help us see our situation more clearly if we just ask them.

The solution to end suffering begins with using this Big 3: Decision Making Framework for Change. We become aware of a problem, determine that our behavior is not working for us, and have freedom to make choices. We have a choice to get out of Hell and end the suffering. We have a choice to be free and at peace with ourselves and the world. We have a choice to live and enjoy life to its full potential. We have a choice to experience joy; joy that exists daily, not a temporary glimpse of it.

Abe Lincoln said, "I think people are as happy as they choose to be." My experience says that this is basically true if the choice is followed up with Action. There needs to be movement towards the solution.

"We will choose free will." – "Free Will" Rush

CHAPTER 6

ENEMY COMBAT

We can't combat The Enemy if we are not aware of Its presence. We have to be vigilant and listen for Its lies. If I hear in my head "I'm not good enough," "I don't do enough," or "I don't have enough," The Enemy is present. When we are aware of The Enemy's presence then we can combat Its deception.

I became aware of this strategy for Enemy Combat from Glen Kelly, an older gentleman at Advent Lutheran Church in Charlotte. He taught me that Embracing the WE is the primary defense against The Enemy. He said, "When The Enemy is trying to lie to you, call It into the light. Tell It to run back to Its hole. Tell It you belong to the light." In addition to Glen's words sometimes I say these words out loud, "I belong to the light. Get lost, Enemy. Leave me alone. I am not going to believe your lies."

After we call The Enemy into the light, It scurries back to Its hole in the darkness. It can't stay in the light of the truth. This works the majority of the time. But, it can only work if I am first aware that I am listening to or believing The Enemy. Calling The Enemy out may also need to be repeated.

Remember, the most serious Enemy lie is when we hear, "There is no reason to keep on living. It's hopeless." This is just a lie, but a powerful one. It appears very real in the moments when The Enemy is winning. I combat this lie by saying, "My life does matter! _____ (name the person) will miss me. Tomorrow is a new day." I pray that you and I don't believe any life threatening lies anymore."

It is my experience that The Enemy is persistent and will lie to us again and again. It will try to deceive us when we are the most vulnerable. That is when we are alone and don't expect it. Life was good in the early years of sobriety. I was celebrating the day. I was sincerely grateful. However in time, I got lost. The Enemy planted lies again, and I believed them. I lost my way. I created Invisible Landmines without knowing it. The Landmines were based on how I thought life should go. I thought my efforts would produce results. These results would make me happy. When results didn't come, then I was prey to misery. A vicious cycle continued over and over again. I was suffering in the dark quagmire with The Enemy, my constant companion. Those closest to me suffered also. How could they not? This is what depression looks like. I was depressed.

When I became aware that The Enemy was winning again and that my way wasn't working, I needed to make a choice to do something different. I decided to get serious about my Landmine Navigation and Embracing the WE. We must respect The Enemy's power of deception. However, we need to constantly be in alert mode in order to combat The Enemy and Its lies at the first sign of Its presence.

"Hello darkness my old friend. I've come to talk with you again." – "Sounds of Silence" Simon and Garfunkel

"Do not give the devil a foothold." Ephesians 4:27

CHAPTER 7

THE PRESENT: DAILY LIVING (THE GAME OF TODAY)

Recovering our freedom, peace, and joy is a process. It is not a one-time event. If we practice using our tools in order to develop skills in Landmine Navigation we will recover in time. We will have setbacks. However, if we don't quit and continue to practice these necessary new skills, we will recover our freedom, peace, and joy. Show me a winner, and I will show you a loser who didn't quit!

We were created to have peace. However, our lack of skills in Landmine Navigation has caused us pain and disrupted our peace. We all want to recover our peace whether we know it or not. The objective is to get back to our original factory setting of freedom, peace, and joy. This is possible.

Most people are familiar with the saying, "One Day at a Time." In my personal experience, it has been a lifesaving concept. I like to call One Day at A Time: The Game of Today. I like to think of each day as a game. Games are supposed to be enjoyable as well as challenging. I took life too seriously for too long. Over time I have learned and adjusted to view life as more of a game. It works for me to view life this way. Each day is like an 18 hole round of golf. It is not a tournament, a season, or a single shot. We can manage our lives better when we stay inside the confines of today.

Inside The Game of Today is a series of moments. Living in each moment is living in the NOW. I call this concept One Shot at a Time. In golf, there is a process that goes into the hitting of each shot. All I am trying to do is Live in the NOW, one moment at a time.

We will have more peace by taking on the day One Shot at a Time. We accomplish this by taking Action on the next right thing in front of us. This eliminates distractions and helps us to DO NO HARM. Taking Action One Shot at a Time simplifies the Game of Today. This concept works. Some days will be peaceful, and other days our peace will be disturbed. There is a process for recovering our peace whenever we notice that it is disturbed.

For me, life can be very overwhelming at times. There are a whole host of reasons for this. Mostly I encounter Invisible Landmines, those Enemy lies that I believe. My peace is disturbed. The lies cause fear. Then I try to manage the fear, and very quickly I am out of this concept of One Shot at a Time. Because I know I will encounter Landmines in The Game of Today, I need to prepare each morning before the game begins, just like I prepare for a round of golf.

BEGINNING EACH DAY (MORNING RITUAL)

We need to develop a routine to start each day for the best chance of success. My Morning Ritual prepares me for Enemy Combat and Landmine Navigation. It doesn't matter where the routine occurs. It is ideal if you are alone in a peaceful setting. However, it is critical that you prepare as early in the day as you can before engaging other humans or jumping into the day. For me, my discipline begins with my first cup of coffee and viewing nature from my screened porch. I have learned to get up earlier and schedule time with myself. Doing this ritual increases my chances of having a great day.

The two main components of The Morning Ritual are Embracing the Vertical We through prayer and meditation and reviewing a personal Vision Document. Through prayer, I surrender to God and hand over all things that we cannot control. I review the important things in my life via my customized Vision Document. Then I am ready to face the day!

EMBRACING THE VERTICAL WE

We prepare for daily Enemy Combat and Landmine Navigation by asking the Vertical WE for help. Each morning, we need to make a decision to let God be the pilot of our life today. We detach from the results. We surrender. The idea is to hand over all the things that I cannot control. Our chances of doing damage are increased without adequate preparation. Being right spiritually assists us to accept things that are out of our control instead of overreacting and causing harm to ourselves and others.

Prayer is communicating with the Vertical WE, with the Higher Power, or with the God of My Understanding. It is a decision to ask the Higher Power for help instead of going it alone. Prayer is like talking to our best friend or father and includes thanking God for our blessings.

GRATITUDE PRAYER

Our first prayer of the Morning Ritual is expressing gratitude for this day. The more sincere we are, the greater connection we will have with our Creator.

"Thank you, Father for this day. Waking up to this day is truly a gift. I thank you for this gift. I will honor this gift by trying to Live in the NOW, trying not to hurt myself or others, practicing Self-Care, and celebrating the day!

OFFERING PRAYER

I start my day by offering myself to my Higher Power. My Creator gave me this life. I am choosing to give it back. I choose to let go of control and let God be the boss, throughout the Game of Today. My job is to not sit around and wait for God. I still need to take Action in love and service to others. The results of the day are not mine.

"God, you gave me this day. I am choosing to give it back. God, you are in charge of this journey. I am in charge of my actions, but you are I charge of the results. We are together in it, but I am in the passenger seat."

LANDMINE REMOVAL PRAYER

"Please, God, remove all Landmines from my path. Please especially remove those I create myself out of my selfishness, fear, sadness, anger or disillusionment. I ask for removal of these Landmines because I realize these are my Landmines today. I am aware of them. I have accepted them. Now I am taking Action on them by Embracing the Vertical WE."

PEACE, GUIDANCE, AND STRENGTH PRAYER

"God, I ask that you please give me peace, guidance, and strength for today's work. I ask for peace of mind to be able to recognize The Enemy's lies. Please give me guidance to handle new Landmines and strength to take Action on navigating them."

I promise you will receive answers if you sincerely ask for The Big Guy's help. This is my experience. Sometimes, I think this is why we have pain or He allows pain, so we can come to him like a little child.

PRAYER FOR OTHERS

"God, I also ask for the same peace, guidance, and strength for the important people in my life, like my family, clients, and friends in difficult situations."

Christians at my church and my mother are really good at this, and they have developed a daily discipline. Each day I pray for my family members, friends, their families, and my clients. I can't promise the results. But I am not praying for specific results other than peace, guidance, and strength. These are the same things I ask for and always get for myself.

MEDITATION

Meditation is designed to find the NOW. It comes in many forms like contemplation. However, I am primarily talking about Transcendental Meditation. Transcendental Meditation is used to quiet the mind. It is a tool used to decrease The Enemy within and increase the GOD spark within us. I am not a meditation expert, however it sounds way more elusive than it really is. It is simply sitting comfortably, closing our eyes, and focusing on our breathing. Breathe in, breathe out. We are trying to clear our mind of Landmines. We are trying to be in the NOW. After 5 to 15 minutes of mediation we will have a clearer mind than when we started. We will be better equipped to recognize The Enemy's presence and hear our own intuitive (God) voice within us.

During meditation, we also listen. I can't claim to have heard a lot of direct messages during my meditation time. My messages usually come out of nowhere during the day. They come when I am in the NOW. Again, I am not an expert. I have made progress in this area, and it is an opportunity for growth. I do claim to have received countless messages through others, songs, and signs. The messages are everywhere as is the God of My Understanding. It makes sense that these coincidences occur because we are all connected. I ask a question, and get an answer some time down the road if I am not blocked off from the good stuff by a Landmine.

VISION DOCUMENT

The Vision Document is a customized plan that is designed as a reminder of the important things in our life. It is important to create a unique Vision Document to prepare for the day. A Vision Document might include: Goals, Gratitude List, Core Principles, Daily Checklist, Assets, Liabilities, Template Schedule, and other key reminders. It should also include anything else you feel is important to your daily success. All of our daily decisions, actions, and thoughts should serve us by moving us closer to our goal of freedom, peace and joy. By reviewing this Vision Document each morning, we have a better chance of having a successful day.

GOALS: NORTH STAR, DO NO HARM AND PRACTICE SELF-CARE

NORTH STAR

A North Star goal is the goal of my life. All decisions throughout the day should serve this goal. For example, twenty years ago my North Star was my happy and healthy together family unit. Whatever decisions I made needed to align with preserving and benefiting my wife and children. Today, my life has changed. My children are older, and I am divorced.

My new North Star is to have joy. Every daily decision either moves me closer to joy or away from it. I try to make decisions that move me closer to joy. Without this North Star, I am directionless and will not make the best decisions towards obtaining what I want.

DO NO HARM TO SELF OR OTHERS

Focusing on ourselves and our priorities is putting first things first. When the plane is going down, we are instructed to put the oxygen mask on ourselves first. We focus on ourselves first. If we do this, we are in a better positon to DO No HARM. A successful day in my world is if I don't drink, don't die, and don't hurt anybody. It seems like a modest objective, but it isn't. The day will be successful if this task is accomplished.

PRACTICE SELF-CARE

Practicing proper Self-Care leads us to freedom, peace, and joy. This objective includes getting right spiritually, physically, and mentally. When practicing Self-Care, we get right spiritually first, then the rest follows.

We need to take care of our physical bodies. If we feel good physically, we are in a better position to feel good mentally. We need to be responsible for our own daily Self-Care. Did we eat properly today? Did we exercise like stretching, walking, weightlifting, or a doing a sport for at least 30 minutes? Did we brush our teeth today? Did we take any medications as properly prescribed? (Sometimes we do need brain chemical adjustments. Meds might be helpful, and one should consult a doctor.) Did we avoid harmful substances? My body is God's house, not mine. Am I taking care of God's house?

If we take care of our spiritual and physical needs, we should be feeling pretty good. Then it will be much easier to take care of our mental needs of making choices and learning new skills.

"I love me." -- "I Love Me" Meghan Trainor

PUTTING ON OUR DAILY ARMOR

The final part of daily preparation is arming ourselves with the three main tools of Acceptance, Forgiveness, and Action. It is like putting on a spiritual suit of armor made of Acceptance. When Landmines appear they don't hurt as much because they can't penetrate the armor. When we are armed with Acceptance, it is easier to accept things we cannot change. I visualize carrying a shield of Forgiveness and a sword of Action. This shield protects me when others try to harm me. If I can forgive them, then I free myself. The sword represents taking Action. I use it to cut through The Enemy's lies and take life One Shot at a Time.

I am now ready to take my Game of Today from the preparation area to the first tee. I am ready to engage other human beings. I am ready to take on the day. I have Embraced the Vertical WE, reviewed my Vision Document, and put my armor on.

Putting on Daily Armor Ephesians 6: 10-17

LANDMINE NAVIGATION (THROUGHOUT THE DAY)

We are now armed with Acceptance, Forgiveness, and Action. We start taking Action by doing One Shot at a Time. We are focusing on the task at hand while attempting to love and serve others. We are practicing the Golden Rule. We are treating others the way we want to be treated. At a minimum, we are trying to DO NO HARM to others and ourselves. This is One Shot at a Time. By doing for others, we get out of ourselves. We want to get out of ourselves because that is where The Enemy tries to live and lies to us. When we are thinking and doing for others, we are free from The Enemy. It goes back to the Golden Rule of loving God and others. When I try to show my love and gratitude for God, I serve His children. **I never have a problem if I am thinking about you instead of me.** I am free from the bondage of pain when I am thinking of someone else or doing for others. At a minimum, we try to DO NO HARM.

Sometimes it is hard to discern what the next right shot is, but we usually know what the next wrong shot is. We obviously try not to do that. If we aren't sure what the next right shot is, we Embrace the WE and ask for help.

Sometimes we have a great day and don't need to navigate Landmines. However, this is rare. Most days will need some Landmine Navigation.

How do you know if you need Landmine Navigation? Something will cause us to feel a disturbance in our peace. We have thoughts, feelings, and emotions that interfere with our goal of freedom, peace and joy. Landmines will happen throughout the day. The Enemy will lie to us. We will believe and act on this belief, causing pain. Others may hurt us. What do we do?

Landmine Navigation starts with Awareness. We can't make any adjustments to our attitude or behavior if we aren't aware. But now we notice our peace is disturbed. Something has happened to disturb our peace. It might not even be a real event. It might just be an Enemy lie, but when we become agitated or frustrated we are in danger of hurting ourselves or others. We have lost our peace. If we don't grab a tool to navigate the Landmine then we will be slaves to our pain. We are not free.

As soon as we become aware of the disturbance in our peace, our first reaction needs to be STOP. We need to call a TIME OUT. We do this so we are in less danger of hurting ourselves or others by over reacting. Our first priority needs to be getting out of danger. We might need to exit the situation if it involves others. We Embrace the Vertical WE and ask for peace, guidance, and strength.

By taking the day One Shot at a Time and practicing this daily process of navigating Landmines, we can quickly recover our freedom, peace, and joy. We can get back to doing the next right shot and celebrating our day.

DAILY PROCESS FOR LANDMINE NAVIGATION WHEN WE HAVE A DISTURBANCE IN OUR PEACE

1) Become aware of the Landmine. (Something has disturbed our peace and we are in danger of harming self or another.)
2) STOP, take a TIME OUT, and just simply breathe. (Get undisturbed and out of danger.)
3) Identify the Landmine by asking, "What caused the disturbance?" and "Why was it caused?" (Introspection questions)

4) Take responsibility for our own freedom, peace, and joy by asking, "What is my part in the disturbance?" We always have a part. "Was my part selfish, fearful or delusional?"

5) Ask, "Is there anything I can do about it?" If the answer is "No," then Acceptance is the answer. If the answer is "Yes," then Action is the answer.

6) Embrace the Vertical and/or Horizontal WE in order to mentally prepare and return to taking the day One Shot at a Time.

This process of Landmine Navigation consists of making spiritual and attitudinal adjustments. Who doesn't need an adjustment? The chiropractor says, "Come on in for an adjustment." Car tires need alignment, which is an adjustment. The football coach talks about how the team needs to make halftime adjustments. What happens if we don't make an adjustment? The back of the Chiropractor's patient will continue to be painful, and the patient will suffer. The tires will wear out quicker. The football team will lose.

We are simply making adjustments to our attitude, our state of mind, One Shot at a Time throughout the Game of Today as a disturbance to our peace occurs. If we can navigate these Landmines successfully without doing harm to ourselves or others then we are back on our way to accomplishing our daily goals and celebrating today.

Sometimes we need to start our day over! When we have gone through the Landmine Navigation process and are still disturbed, then we need a reboot of our day. We need to stop. We need to go back to the Morning Ritual and begin again as if we just got up. Sometimes we need to utilize additional tools in the toolbox like: Forgiveness, Burden Sharing, and the God Box.

Navigating Landmines is a process. The skill of learning to live successfully One Shot at a Time does not come overnight. It takes practice and more practice. We will NOT do it perfectly. However, if we practice, we will make progress. Over time, we will look back and see that we have recovered our freedom, peace, and joy by trying to DO NO HARM to ourselves or others and by practicing Self-Care. After this skill becomes a natural part of our day, we find joy! We find that this attitude adjustment works! We are recovering One Shot at a Time!

CLOSING THE DAY (REFLECTION)

In closing the day, we count our blessings. They are abundant. It truly is amazing how wonderful life is, and how fortunate we all are to have experienced the gift of living the day. Win or lose, are we thankful for it?

At the end of each day we review all that happened. How was my Enemy Combat? Was I aware of The Enemy? When aware, did I Accept the situation or did I take Action? Did I Embrace the WE? Or did The Enemy win today's battle?

We will lose some battles of the day. It's ok. Some days are bad and just need to end. Tomorrow is full of promise as long as we don't quit. When The Game of Today is over, it's over. If you played well, take time to enjoy it.

"Celebrate today!" Walt Disney

CHAPTER 8

PAST: GETTING PAST THE PAST

INTROSPECTION

For many of us, we have been unaware of The Enemy's foothold in us for years. This foothold has manifested in our fears, resentments, sadness, selfishness, and delusion. Getting past the past requires specific introspection and analysis. Time needs to be set aside to work on this. We need to identify old hurts and angers. Once identified, we need to use tools with the help of the Vertical and Horizontal WE in order to have a chance of being successful in leaving the past behind us. Using a golf analogy, we still need to play our daily round of golf, but our long term project is improving our swing mechanics. Getting past the past is a similar long term project.

Introspection is a tool for analyzing old hurts, fears and angers that are recurring patterns that disturb our peace. Reviewing our fears is an important task. This is how we uncover fear Invisible Landmines. Take out a piece of paper and draw a line down the middle creating two columns. In the first column, ask, "What are we afraid of?" In the second column, ask "Why?" Then we write all of our fears down as well as the reasons why. When we review our fears, we find that we are afraid of a lot of things, like being afraid of failing or of hitting a bad golf shot. You name it, we are afraid. We find out that we don't trust ourselves and don't trust God. Most importantly, we find out that many of these fears are Invisible Landmines that we didn't know existed. The fears are The Enemy's lies that we are believing. We may have been believing them for years.

After completing this exercise about our fears, we list them in our Vision Document to be reviewed daily. Embrace the WE. We share our fears with God and another human being. This decreases their power. We ask the Vertical WE for strength.

Resentments can be uncovered in introspection also. A resentment is replayed anger. If we get angry today then replay that anger tomorrow, it is called a resentment. We are resending it. This is a "dis-ease." Resentment has caused me more suffering than anything else. It has caused others much pain also. Sometimes we choose to not take Action, and we don't navigate a Landmine. We choose not to heal, and instead, we stay angry. We try to wish the resentments away. However, resentments don't get wished away. They don't go away on their own. Resentments must be dealt with for healing to occur. If not resolved, resentments become Invisible Landmines again and again. Thus, suffering continues.

This is how we uncover resentment Invisible Landmines. Take out a piece of paper and draw a line down the middle creating two columns. In the first column, ask, "Who are we mad at?" In the second column, ask "Why? What did they do?"

FORGIVENESS

After completing this exercise and the resentment is clearer, now what do we do? Again, we place any uncovered Landmines in our Vision Document to review daily. Then we must forgive those who hurt us. Forgiveness is necessary if we want to be free from the past. It is all about our own freedom. Do I want to be free or not?

People are not perfect. We make mistakes. We are self-centered and living in our delusion of separateness from God and each other. We are spiritually sick. So, starting with sincere pity for those who hurt us is where forgiveness begins. Simply say a prayer stating that you forgive them. I say this to God and myself: "I forgive you and feel sorry for you." I need to remember that the majority of the time these individuals don't have effective Enemy Combat skills. They are probably dealing with their own Invisible Landmines of which they are unaware. If the past hurt caused a resentment and still exists the day after you forgave the person, then pray for strength and repeat the exercise. If you can't get past this, it is suggested that you reach out to the Horizontal WE and lighten your burden.

SPIRITUAL TRUTH

We have now forgiven someone who hurt us and caused our resentment. It is a spiritual truth that when my peace is disturbed there is ALWAYS a part I played. This is true 100% of the time. In the past, we blamed someone else, probably the person we just forgave. Now, if we are honest, and by using the introspection questions, we can determine our part in the disturbance. We can take ownership of our problems. We also can become aware of our Landmines which have been blocking us off from freedom for years. We can accept that often we are in our own way, and that The Enemy has been winning for a long time. Little growth can occur if we blame others or God. No more making excuses! It's time to take a look inside of us and be responsible for our own actions which caused the pain and suffering.

Returning to the introspection exercise, turn the paper over and focus on uncovering our part in the recurring disturbance. Ask, "What was our part? Was it selfish, fearful, or delusional?"

What happens if we can't see our part? Or we didn't do anything wrong and are a victim? How can it be true then that we always (100% of the time) have a part? Usually our part is that we expected others to not hurt us. We had an Invisible Landmine of expectation of how life was supposed to go and how others were supposed to treat us. We were the ones who created this expectation. This is how we always have a part in our own disturbance.

CONFESSION

After answering the questions and uncovering our part, it is time to Embrace the WE. We confess what our part was by telling God and another human being. If we don't confess our part, we will continue to be blocked off from peace and suffering will continue.

Forgiving ourselves is also important. We have been trying to get past the past. We cannot accomplish this if we don't forgive our own transgressions. Of course, we can't forgive our own transgressions if we are unaware of them. This is why introspection is important to uncover them. After we confess them, we are forgiven. God loves us unconditionally. God forgives anyone who confesses their sins with sincerity. However, we must attempt to change and not repeat the same problem behavior. We have been trying to get past the past and have a fresh start.

RESTITUTION

If in the process of introspection we find that we have hurt someone then we need to make restitution to them. We need to do this in order to be forgiven and free from the past. We are attempting the clear the slate of the past. It is important to ask forgiveness directly from those we hurt. We also ask what Action we can take to make things right with them. Some call these amends, like mending a fence.

Sometimes I have found that when I attempt to make restitution, the person is surprised that I bring up the perceived hurt. They either have no memory of the incident, or the incident was not nearly as big a deal to them as it was to me. It's very unfortunate that I had been carrying this burden for a long time. It was not only unnecessary, but it wasn't even reality.

Introspection, forgiveness, confession and restitution will transform us into new and better version of ourselves. We cannot accomplish ultimate freedom, peace, and joy unless we get past the past.

"And be kind to one another, tenderhearted, forgiving one another, even as God in Christ forgave you. Ephesians 4:32

"If we confess our sins, He is faithful and just and will forgive us our sins and purify us from all unrighteousness." 1 John 9:11

COMMON LANDMINES

The following are common Landmines that we may uncover during introspection. After we are aware of these common Landmines, we have a choice to navigate them or not. We ask ourselves "Are the Landmines working for us? Or are they not?" They usually aren't if we are able to be honest with ourselves. The solution to conquering these past Landmines is always Embracing the WE and the Willingness to take Action navigating them.

MY LANDMINES

Through introspection, I uncovered these personal Landmines: fears, resentments, sadness, selfishness, and delusion. My Landmines cause me to overreact, blame others, and try to control things. I am inconsiderate, entitled, impatient, perfectionistic, discontented, judgmental, and overly sensitive to what others say and do. I take life too seriously. I have a tendency to be negative and go it alone at times. Sometimes, I play God because I don't trust God. These are some of my Landmines that I need to navigate. The good news is after proper introspection I am aware of the Landmines. All the Landmines have decreased in power when treated spiritually One Shot at a Time. However, they don't go away. This is the human condition. The Landmines intensify if my spiritual condition deteriorates. They don't interfere with my freedom, peace, and joy nearly as much as they used to when I wasn't aware of them.

The Navajo Indians weave an intentional imperfection into each garment or blanket to remind themselves of their human condition. That is just beautiful to me.

We have a gum tree in our back yard. The tree is tall, beautiful, and alive. It is light. It is simply being. It survives on what nature gives it. It is dependent on a Higher Power for its life. Every early spring it grows leaves and little gum balls. Later in spring it drops its prickly gum balls. I was in Hell one day, and I decided to cut the tree down. Fortunately, the next day, after sleeping on it, I changed my mind. It dawned on me that perhaps God put that gum tree there for me to get a reminder of my own gums (Landmines). Would God cut me down? The next time the gums fell, I cheerfully picked up about 500 gums with the understanding that I probably have about 500 Landmines that cause pain in my relationships.

PRIDE (EGO)

Pride leads the way in the sin category. Pride tells me that I don't have a problem. Pride tells me I don't need help from God or others. Therefore, we go it alone making us susceptible to The Enemy. This blocks us from the source of the solution, The WE.

Pride says, "I got this. I don't need any help. I don't need to Embrace the WE. I can handle it myself. I don't have a problem; therefore, I don't need a solution." So, what's the solution here? Unfortunately, there isn't one until the pain of our pride causes us to become aware that our way is not working. Then, we can choose to do something different like choosing to Embrace the WE and other Core Principles.

SELFISHNESS

We are all selfish at times. It is a part of the human condition. I have found that the majority of the time we act selfishly out of fear. This selfishness is our reaction to fear. We react instead of accepting things that we cannot change. We retaliate instead of forgiving. We forget that the fear we are feeling usually is an Enemy lie and not even real. This selfishness hurts others, and then in turn they react and retaliate. It is a vicious cycle that could have been eliminated had we not reacted selfishly in the first place. We need to take the lead and act unselfishly. Someone needs to. Why not us?

WRATH (ANGER)

Who hasn't been angry? I am so fortunate that my girls have never seen me drink, but I regret they sure have seen me angry. I've been angry at them, angry at their mother, angry at the world, and angry with God. I have been angry at how they treated me, didn't respect me, and were selfish. I've been angry that life wasn't fair, or at least that's how I perceived it treated me. I perceived that life wronged me. I didn't have the skills I have now to handle this anger. Sadly, it is the chief reason my marriage of 26 years eventually failed. We would replay the same old hurts, resentments, and angers. We both did this to each other.

ENVY (JEALOUSY)

Who doesn't want what others have: money, fame, time, or relationships? Is there anything I can do about what you have? NO, so why am I wasting my own time coveting what you have or being angry that you have these things? Why don't I choose to focus on what I can control and take Action towards obtaining the things that I want? Is it really even true that these things I am jealous of will even make me happy? The Enemy lies to me telling me, "If I only had a house like they have, I would be happy." Material things only bring temporary happiness.

GLUTTONY

"All things should be in moderation." That's an old saying, right? I agree with this saying, assuming, I can actually act in moderation. If I know that I can't act in moderation then I shouldn't even attempt the action at all. This was my case when drinking alcohol. I also have been known from time to time to chow down a whole can of Pringles.

GREED

I will be happy when I reach the top. When I have enough money to _____? How much is enough? Is there ever enough?

"Never Enough" The Cure

LUST

Lust is defined as a strong craving for something: lust for power, lust for a beautiful person, lust for a substance. When thinking about something turns into a mental obsession, we are dealing with lust.

"Throw off your old sinful nature and your former way of life, which is corrupted by lust and deception." Ephesians. 4:22

GUILT

I used to feel guilty about what I had done. But I also felt guilt about what I had left undone. Guilt occupied my mind keeping me from the NOW. I was a slave to my guilt until I used the tools of introspection, confession, and restitution to get past the past of guilt. Today, if I am taking life One Shot at a Time properly I should be guilt free. A small example of this is seeing litter on the ground. I used to ignore it. Today I can't go by litter and not pick it up. This way I don't feel new guilt from leaving something undone.

SADNESS

We all have been sad. It is inevitable. Life disappoints us sometimes. Others hurt us. It is when this sadness carries over into the following days or weeks or years that it becomes a recurring Landmine requiring serious action to remove.

"Poor me! Life doesn't treat me fairly. God is out to get me again." This is a Landmine to expect life to go my way all the time. Sure, life has its disappointments. Grief and sadness are painful and inevitable. However, if I stay in the sadness instead of Embracing the WE, then I fall prey to suffering in my own self-pity.

SLOTH (LAZINESS)

When I don't take Action on something that I should, that is sloth. The man in the mirror (internal judge) beats me up, and others who are holding me accountable (parents, bosses, daughters, spouse) are on my back. I am currently not working out as much as I want or drinking a daily double spinach fruit smoothie as planned. I would be happier if I just did healthy things. Then The Enemy would not have the opportunity to tell me how much of a slacker I am; and the reality is, I would be physically healthier. I would feel better. I would have better results because I was happier. So, we should simply choose to go do what we don't want to do One Shot at a Time.

FEAR (ANXIETY)

We all experience fear. The question is: How are we going to react to it? Perhaps these acronyms for "FEAR" explain our choices with it. We can "Fuck Everything And Run," or we can "Face Everything And Recover." We need to remember that The Enemy's only weapon is to deceive us. In that case, "FEAR" stands for False Events Appearing Real. It is our choice if we believe the lies. It is always our choice.

Today even though I still have many fears, they have decreased. This is because I have written them down and reviewed them. The fears have been brought into the light. I am on my way to freedom, peace, and joy by living One Shot at a Time.

Fear can be an asset if it motivates us in a healthy direction. When fear freezes us into immobility of thought or action, it turns into anxiety. I feared I was going to lose my family and go off the deep end if I didn't address my drinking. However, fear is also what drives us to hurt others and ourselves. I have found over the years that the majority of my fears are not even real. Again, Fear=False Events Appearing Real. Fears are lies from The Enemy. They are Invisible Landmines that I don't even know exist until I step on them. Most of my fears begin with me thinking about me and trying to control the future and trying to control outcomes and results. It was the #1 reason I wasn't a better golfer when I was younger. I would fear hitting the ball in the water or out of bounds and try to control the shot more. The more I tried to manage the shot, the worse it got. When I didn't get the results I desired, I tried harder. The same results followed. Fear seems to be in our DNA. I believe we were created this way with our instincts for survival. The question is do our fears work for us?

CHAPTER 9

FUTURE: JOYFUL LIVING

If we have thoroughly cleansed our past, we are free. We have peace. We now have a better opportunity for maximum joy. We are living in the NOW. We are trying to take life One Shot at a Time. We are following the Golden Rule by displaying it in our actions. We are motivated to take Action and serve others. We are thinking and doing for others. Some days we won't be able to reach that goal of loving and serving others. It is ok because it is Progress not perfection. On these days, we simply strive to DO NO HARM to others or ourselves.

We are free from the guilt that used to haunt us. We have paid for our past and are forgiven. We have a lot of hope because we are feeling good. We are experiencing the promise of actually seeing God because we have purified our past. We don't suffer new guilt because we aren't harming others and we aren't leaving necessary things undone. We are taking life on life's terms instead of our own terms. We aren't overreacting to tiny things. We have learned how to successfully take life One Shot at a Time because we have been trained through daily disciplines inside the confines of The Game of Today.

The future takes care of itself when we learn how to live in the present moment successfully. Our goal of freedom, peace, and joy awaits us in the future when get past the past and develop daily living skills. The colors are brighter. We accept things that are out of our control more easily. Our thoughts are more focused. We are free. We know peace. We enter the world of the spirit! We are alive!

"Try and enjoy the here and now, the future will take care of itself somehow."— "Life in One Day" Howard Jones

One of the other benefits of getting past the past is we know ourselves better. We must first know who we are not, in order to discover who we are. We are not God. We are children of God. I am not God, but God is in me. We have uncovered some Landmines, like our selfishness in our human condition. We are watchful so we don't cause ourselves or others harm. We are trying to learn from our past mistakes. When we make new mistakes, we go through the process of Landmine Navigation in order to be free and of maximum service to others. If we are stuck in the darkness, we Embrace the WE and engage in a new Introspection and analysis.

"Those who fail to learn from history are condemned to repeat it." Winston Churchill

We have unblocked our consciousness which allows clearer communication with the Vertical WE. We can feel and believe we are closer to our Creator. We can sometimes hear our little God voice within where our intuitive thoughts occur.

When we get past the past and develop a discipline for daily living, we are decreasing The Enemy within. We are also increasing the little piece of God within us too. When we do this we are getting unblocked. We are growing into the image of our Creator. We begin to become aware of our intuitive thought. We realize it had been there the whole time but now we can hear it. This is our little God voice within. Ever heard anyone ask you, "What does your gut tell you to do?" This is an example of it.

"Let your conscience be your guide." Jiminy Crickett

"Does your conscience bother you? Tell the truth." – "Sweet Home Alabama" Lynyrd Skynyrd

We have recovered from the past by overcoming some of our biggest landmines. However, we are still in recovery because recovery is a moment by moment thing. We are like swimming ducks on a pond. We appear calm on the surface but we are paddling under the water always taking Action on what we can control. We can control our Self-Care. We can control how we treat others. We can control how we react to how others treat us and to life's disappointments. This peace will continue as long as we choose to work for it. We continue trying to grow into the image of GOD. We move with the rhythm of life. Life has a natural rhythm like ocean waves or breathing. When I was in Hell instead of Heaven, I was usually moving either faster than the natural rhythm or not at all. We are more at peace when we move in a natural rhythm. We need our pace of life to not move too fast and too slowly.

We strive for balance in our lives. When it is time to work, we work. When it is time to play we play. We take care of our responsibilities, which includes having fun. When a car tire is out of balance it doesn't work properly. The same is true with our life. When our life is out of balance we are more susceptible to The Enemy winning. The main areas of our life are: spiritual, physical, family, work, friends, hobbies, and other areas in our life that need time and energy. We strive to keep things simple. The simpler we can make our life the more freedom, peace, and joy we have. This is my experience.

We are taking life easily. When we apply "Easy does it," we are reminding ourselves to not take life so seriously. We take it easy. We try to live our daily lives like "Easy like Sunday morning." Sunday mornings are gentle. They are not rushed. They are peaceful. I want to live every day with the peace of Sunday morning. I want to swing a golf club this way. I want to treat others this way. I can do this when my spiritual condition is solid and I am Embracing the WE!

"Because I'm easy. Easy like Sunday Morning." -- "Easy" The Commodores

FAITH AND TRUST

Faith is trust. Trust is having faith in what we believe. Trust brings freedom, peace, and joy. When we trust, we are confident. We are in a better positon to be fearless. Trust comes from experience. We have faith in God. We have faith in the daily process of One Shot at a Time.

Here is an example. I am new in town and my car breaks down. I don't know where to take it to get it fixed. So, I ask you. You tell me to take it to Joe, and he will do a good job. I take it to Joe and he does in fact do a good job. My car is fixed. I took it to Joe on your trust of him. The second time my car breaks down. I don't ask you for a recommendation because I know where to take it. I take it to Joe because I have evidence and experience. I have trust and faith that Joe will solve my problem.

So, we go forward about our day and trust that the future will be filled with freedom and peace. We are choosing to make it that way. We trust that we can navigate any Landmines in our way.

JOY

Joy is not just a goal. It is an important part of recovery. When we experience joy, our brain is triggered to produce chemicals that bring us more joy. So experiencing joy brings us even more joy. Joy works!

Rick Warren, founder of the very successful Saddleback Church in Southern California said that his main regret was not having more music as part of his service. Why? Music brings us joy!

Golf, Fantasy Football, pool volleyball, snow skiing/snowboarding with my two girls, walking my dog and hanging out with my friends bring me joy. Krispy Kreme original hot donuts, large vanilla ice cream cones from Dairy Queen, and bacon bring me joy! Loving and serving others is what brings me the most joy of all. Seeing the light come on in someone that I am working with brings me immense joy. What brings you joy? Whatever it is, I pray you seek and experience it!

LAUGHTER

Laughter brings us joy. So make it a priority in your life. Have you ever heard anyone ever say they wish they didn't laugh so much? Old wisdom says, "Laughter is the best medicine." Can anyone really disagree? Make it a priority to laugh more! And I will try to do the same, TODAY!

"Don't hurry, don't worry, and don't forget to smell the flowers." Walter Hagen

HOBBIES (GOLF)

I have been extremely fortunate to have played golf all my life, since I was 7. I became a member of the PGA and a private club pro. It was my dream and life's work to promote the game and its benefits. I was a natural at it. I was on my way to having a great career.

But life happens. Families, responsibilities, and health concerns trump dreams. Life had other plans for me than being a Club Pro. I found my true calling. It is to make God's kids aware of the light and lead them toward it. Golf can play a huge part in this transformational process. It is important that we have joy in our lives. That joy can be found daily in golf or another hobby. A hobby is important for joy. It should be a part of our life balance and physical exercise.

In my experience, there is no greater game that symbolizes life than golf. To learn how to play good golf, one MUST learn how to manage one's self and one's emotions. One must overcome large counterintuitive Invisible Landmines. One must be persistent, because there is nothing harder than golf. Golf will build good character. Just like in life, there aren't any shortcuts in golf. One must develop the discipline of the tedious practice of repetition in order to get good. Learning how to master oneself is a big part of what this journey is all about. Why do you think they call it the Masters?

Golf brings people together. Being connected to others is joyful. Golf brings us nature. Nature brings us joy. Golf brings us exercise. Exercise is joyful. Golf allows us to take a break from our problems and our busy lives. Golf is also challenging. We can compete against ourselves and/or others. Challenge and competition brings us joy. It can be played as a team or individually. Golf can be played on many different courses with hardly ever two shots the same. Golf brings us joy.

Golf doesn't have to be traditional golf either because there are disc golf, foot golf, and lacrosse golf. All types of golf accomplish joy. If golf isn't your thing, then there are plenty of other hobbies that can bring you joy. Finding one that allows you to experience the connection to others, nature, and exercise will bring you joy. Live, Love, laugh, play, work, dance, golf and/or _____. Fill in your own blank. Whatever brings you joy. Healthy joy!

THE MASTERS GOLF TOURNAMENT

What a privilege it is to attend the Masters each year. It is an amazing experience that everyone should do once, if you get the chance. Pimento cheese or egg salad sandwiches for under $2, and souvenir cokes or lemonades for $1. The Masters has free parking and the most beautiful setting imaginable. Watching the Masters brings me joy. The winners have perfected how to be Masters of themselves that week. This is truly a gift to experience. Thank you, Augusta National and Bobby Jones. The Masters in person or on the TV brings me joy.

PETS

Pets bring us joy. Roxie was our family dog from Christmas 2006 until fall of 2017. What a Christmas gift she was. She showed our family what unconditional love was. She was always at the door waiting for me when I got home. We rescued her from Project Halo here in Charlotte. The truth is she rescued me. Roxie was an Australian cattle dog who hopped like a deer. She caught Frisbees. Roxie would herd the girls and nip on their heels when they played because she thought it was her job. It was a very sad day when she died. Roxie brought us a lot of joy. I hope you find joy wherever you can and appreciate it while you have it.

CHAPTER 10

MORE THOUGHTS AND TOOLS

TIMEOUT: EASY DOES IT

Sometimes a simple tool can save the day! Timeout is such a tool. Taking a Timeout is a way to change our challenging place to a safer place until we calm down or get control of ourselves. We can buy time to choose a pathway to navigate a Landmine. We take a Timeout so we don't create a bigger problem or additional Landmines by overreacting or reacting rashly. We should take a timeout when we have a disturbance in our peace. It's all about our reaction when we see or hit an Invisible Landmine. Do we get angry? Sad? Scared? Do we fight it? Pretend it's not there? Or do we accept it is there and needs to be navigated? We take time for Self-Care and try to get back to the NOW where peace can be found. This is where we are free from the emotions that block us off from feeling peace. We are free to not make mountains out of molehills. If we choose not to navigate the Landmines, we stay stuck on the problem instead of the solution.

ROW, ROW, ROW YOUR BOAT

A vision of our future is summed up pretty well in this childhood nursery rhyme. "Row, row, row your boat, Gently down the stream, Merrily,

merrily, merrily, Life is but a dream." This children's song teaches us life lessons. This song is so simple that the solutions for life were right in front of us and being taught to us when we were just little tikes.

Rowing is Action. So it could easily read Action, Action, Action.

"Your boat" indicates that the boat is mine. It doesn't say take Action on someone else's boat. It says to take Action on MY boat. Take Action on what I can control. Stay inside my boundary, inside my own hula hoop. I only have control over my attitude and my reaction to life.

It says "gently." It doesn't say hastily, impulsively, angrily, with frustration, or with sadness. It says gently, like a gentleman. Row gently with ease and row "down the stream," not up the stream. Row with the current not against it. Take the easy path, not the difficult path. Go with the flow. Easy does it.

"Merrily, merrily, merrily" means to be at peace, to be free, to be grateful for the moment, and to be in pursuit of happiness.

"Life is but a dream." Life really is short, isn't it? Time goes faster and faster every year as I get older. We really are only here on this moving rock as this person for a very short time. It is like a dream.

"I'm older now, but I am still running against the wind." – "Against the Wind" Bob Seger

SPIRITUALLY FIT

When I am spiritually fit, life is like bumper cars. My car collides with others but there is no damage. I am quick to accept things that I cannot change. I am quick to forgive others when they hurt me. However, when I am not on top of my spiritual game and when my car collides with others, there is damage. Then it is demolition derby, not bumper cars.

Unfortunately, when I am not spiritually fit, I have a tendency to see my problems as larger than they really are. It's like I am pole vaulting over mouse turds. A mouse turd is very small, usually just like most of my problems. However, I see the mouse turd as a huge problem requiring a pole vault to get over. Making a mountain out of a molehill is a common saying for the same thing.

I have found that what I think about grows. If I am thinking about the problem it grows. If I am thinking about the solution, it grows. Why would any sane person choose to think about the problem? He wouldn't unless he was unaware of The Enemy or was unskilled in navigating Landmines. I needed to develop skills to fight The Enemy (which in this case was me) and navigate Landmines (my self-created Landmines). To this day, I am still surprised by Invisible Landmines when I step on them and feel pain. A successful strategy is to keep my expectations low and acceptance high. It is a simple idea but not easy to do.

We are in paradise. We are surrounded by good stuff. However, there is one little bug (problem). Why is it that I have a tendency to focus on the problem instead of the solution? I do this because it is a habit. It's a bad habit that doesn't serve me. It is an opportunity for spiritual growth.

I was heading into a 7:15 am meeting and hadn't had enough coffee. I shut my car door and immediately realized what I had done. I locked the keys in my car again. I laughed and went to my meeting. Then after the meeting, I asked a friend to give me a ride to my house to get my backup set of keys.

Let's compare that to the previous time I did the exact same thing. I was pissed off. I was fearful that I would miss the meeting and that my day would be all screwed up. I was afraid that it would cost me money. The difference between the two similar events was in my spiritual condition. My spiritual condition was solid, and therefore, my reaction was laughter at myself for doing something dumb. When our spiritual cup is full we react with laughter or not at all. When we are spiritually deficient, we react with negative emotions like anger and have a good chance of hurting others and ourselves.

GOD BOX

A God Box is an amazing tool! It can be an actual box or physical place to put our worries and burdens in. First, we write all of our worries and burdens down on paper. Then we place what we have written inside the God Box. It is critical that we let go of the worries so God in the Vertical

WE can handle the results. A God Box doesn't have to be a real tangible object. It is the concept of "Letting Go and Letting God."

A few years ago, I was in Hell, and I was filled with fear. My new business was in crisis. My daughter was in crisis. These two things put my marriage in crisis. Mostly, my actions of self will were compounding the problems. I was trying so hard to manage my problems and finding solutions to my problems by changing the circumstances. When that didn't work, I would try harder and then even harder. I finally had to accept the fact that my way wasn't working. I had to make a choice to surrender and ask for help. I wrote every burden down on paper and put them all in an actual God Box. I detached from the results and gave them to God. The situations didn't change right away, but by taking this Action step I was moving towards the solution. I had more peace and freedom. I reviewed the contents of the God Box a year later. I found that 25 out of 25 burdens that I gave to God had been solved in one way or another. Amazing!

THE FOUR AGREEMENTS

The Four Agreements by Don Ruiz changed my world. The book brought me a clear understanding about how communication breaks down in a relationship. It is a must-read book about relationships that I recommend to my clients. This ancient Toltec wisdom is simple, practical and very enlightening.

Agreement #1: Do Your Best

I didn't know that I was hurting myself and others by not doing my best. "Not doing my best" opened the door for the internal judge (The Enemy) to lie to me. The Enemy told me that I was inadequate and not worthy of good things in life. When I do my best and when I leave it on the field like NFL players talk about, I feel pretty good about myself. I am closer to freedom, peace, and joy.

Agreement #2: Be Impeccable with Your Word

I learned to speak my truth in all my affairs. It was one of the best skills I have developed. My two girls have grown up with a high priority for being honest. It has served my relationship with both of them well.

Agreement #3: Don't Make Assumptions

Well, this is impossible because I now realize I make assumptions all the time. Many times my assumptions are inaccurate, and I have pain as a result. However, I try to not make assumptions.

Agreement #4: Don't Take It Personally

If others are doing their best to speak their truth, we should not take the statements we hear personally. If we do take a statement personally it is on us, not them. We are not being attacked. because we feel attacked.

Well, most of us don't have the skills of The Four Agreements so we are left to do the best unskilled job we can. Can you see the dance of miscommunication that precedes the pain and suffering of a simple communication breakdown? I do my best to tell you my truth, and the recipient takes it personally because they make an assumption?

THE GRIEVING PROCESS

It has always been hard for me to accept the things I can't change. It took me a long time to understand and believe that Acceptance was in fact the only answer to things I can't change. It helped me to learn that Acceptance is the last step in The Five Steps of Grief by Elisabeth Kubler-Ross and David Kessler. I learned that it wasn't just me that was slow to accept things. The more I cared about something, the harder it was to accept it when I didn't get what I wanted. Of course, I can now see that it was my expectations about God and others that was the ultimate Invisible Landmine I created. It was me (and only me) that put myself in a positon to suffer. The stages of this grieving process are very helpful to understand.

1) Denial

Denial is believing the lie that the disturbance, problem, or situation is not real. We pretend the situation does not exist. I was working with a 40 year old man who was told by his doctor that he needed to quit drinking or he would die. His solution to his problem was to get a different doctor. This is denial.

2) Anger

When we accept that the problem is real and that we can't do anything about it, then we become angry. How could God allow this to happen? How could this person cause me pain like this? We are pissed off. The more we care about a situation or the more we want a desired outcome or result, the angrier we are. Of course, the secret is to not react on our anger.

3) Bargaining

We try to change the result of what has already occurred. Looking back, nothing was a clearer example of bargaining than when I wrote my 17 point 4 page letter to my wife explaining why her leaving and deciding to break apart the family unit was a bad Idea. I was trying to talk sense into her after she had already made up her mind. I was bargaining.

4) Sadness

When all my efforts at denial, anger, and bargaining failed, I fell into sadness. The good news about this is after we have felt the sadness, we are close to the end. We are close to Acceptance.

5) Acceptance

Acceptance is the end of the pain and suffering. We are different individuals at this stage then we were when the process started. Hopefully we have grown in the process. We just add it to the long list of life's experiences and move on with gratitude. We are glad we are still here and are now free again to pursue peace and joy along this journey called life.

WHEN GOD DOESN'T GIVE US SOMETHING, IT IS FOR OUR PROTECTION

Sometimes life doesn't give me what I want or when I want it. I have had my share of disappointments, we all have. What has helped me over the years is to remember when life brings me disappointments that perhaps it is GOD's way of trying to protect me. I thought the worst thing that could ever happen to me was to stop drinking and have to ask God (who I wasn't sure existed) for help. I was wrong, totally wrong. What I thought was the worst thing to ever happen to me ended up being the greatest thing that ever happened to me. So, this just proves I really don't know what is best for me. God was protecting me. I believe He is always trying to protect me unless I have a lesson to learn and must experience the pain in order to learn it.

THIS TOO SHALL PASS

"This too shall pass" is a reminder that this difficult moment will not last. It is problematic when we are in the middle of a disturbance to our peace. But no matter how overwhelming it seems, the disturbance does eventually pass. Time will take care of a lot of pain. Sometimes we just need to accept it and keep going with hope that the future will be better.

SLEEP ON IT

Sleeping on a decision is a great tool and is very wise. I have made several bad decisions because they were made too quickly. I should have slept on them. I have also struggled at times to make a decision, but when I woke up the next day the answer was very clear. On a simpler note, Fantasy Football is an important hobby of mine that brings me joy. Trading players is a part of winning. I try to sleep on my decisions in order to make good decisions. This has been learned after years of sometimes making emotional and off-the-cuff poor decisions.

DO I WANT TO BE RIGHT OR DO I WANT TO BE HAPPY?

I spent years wanting to be right. I would argue my point until I was blue in the face. Why did I have this need to be right? If unhappiness with the person I was arguing with was the end result, what did I gain? Today, I would rather be happy than right. It works.

LIVE LIKE YOU ARE DYING

Live like we are dying means to celebrate the day as if it is our last one. Would I really be allowing these Landmines to be disturbing my peace if I were not going to be on this earth tomorrow? I sometimes allow slow and selfish drivers to interfere with my peace. Would I really want to give them the power to take my freedom? Would I worry about any of these pesky daily Landmines if I knew I weren't going to be around tomorrow? Of course not. I would be doing what I want to do. I would be with family and friends. We would be laughing and enjoying the day. The last thing I would be doing is stressing over some other driver and the traffic. However, I still do it, from time to time.

"Live Like I Am Dying" Tim McGraw

Have you ever seen a hearse with a U Haul trailer behind it? I haven't. You can't take the material stuff with you when you go. And by the way, no one gets out alive. So, don't take life so seriously. Enjoy the people in your life. Enjoy the experiences you have.

We are made up of energy particles. The same energy as the Creator. The same energy as water, trees, and everything. Take the leaf for example. It is spring right now, and the tree is full of life. It has new leaves. They grow, turn colors, and then fall. They die. The dead leaf can be crumpled into dust and become Invisible to the eye. My point is that our life in its human form is temporary. It can end at any time. It also will not last forever.

"All we are is dust in the wind." – "Dust in the Wind" Kansas

FLAT TOP

His real name was Steve H. but we called him Flattop because he had a high and tight flattop haircut. It was old school. I had the privilege of coaching him. He was suffering, but after learning the tools in this guide and practicing them he experienced freedom, peace, and joy. He went on to coach others. This was a tremendous joy for me to see. Unfortunately, he was tragically killed in a car accident. As a direct result of his accident, there is now a traffic light at the intersection where his accident happened.

GRAY TWO SOCKS WOLF

Gray Two Socks Wolf is a Cherokee tribal elder. He was the first person I met that had a God-like aura that I could feel. He had a real presence. I didn't know what it was at the time, but I was drawn to it. He was down in Charlotte for cancer treatment. He was on his way back to the mountain reservation to die because the doctors told him that it was terminal. He said "If you are looking in the mirror and don't see the problem then you are heading for a big problem." Of course, here he is talking about The Enemy. He is talking about the human condition and that the problem is within us.

"If you want to make the world a better place take a look in the mirror and make a change. I'm the man in the mirror." -- "Man in the Mirror" Michael Jackson

CHAPTER 11

MORE SPIRITUALITY

YOUR OWN CONCEPT OF GOD

It doesn't matter what I believe. **It only matters what you believe.** You can choose your own concept of God, Father, Universe, Source, Force or whatever you say. You are the boss of you. In fact, you can choose to not believe in a Higher Power, connection to each other, or any type of spirituality. That's ok. That's my point. What is the only thing that truly matters? Are you suffering? Or have you suffered? Or do you know someone who is suffering right now? I bet the answer is "Yes" to at least one of these questions. I believe there is a reason that this message is finding you. Perhaps, you are the light who will carry it to the suffering. It is in the seeking that one finds the truth. In finding the truth, we find ourself.

BIG BANG

In the beginning was God and only God. There was only God and space (void). He couldn't experience himself because there wasn't anything else. He was lonely. So He decided to separate himself. BANG. Separation occurs. Now God can experience God. He can experience himself. He can enjoy himself. He is no longer lonely.

ONENESS

I believe we are spiritual beings having a human experience. I believe we are all part of the ONE. I believe that there is only ONE. I believe we are all connected to it. I believe that we all have a tiny piece of the ONE in all us. We all appear different but deep down we are all the same. We are energy. We are light. We are all connected.

"The world will live as one." – "Imagine" John Lennon

COINCIDENCES

The Celestine Prophecy by James Redfield was a number #1 best seller in the 90's in the Fiction category. However, in my experience, it is nonfiction. It is real. Since we are all connected to each other, it makes perfect sense to ask the Universe a question and get an answer. This has happened to me many times since becoming aware of our oneness and aware of our connectedness. I would ask a question, only to myself. No one else knew it. The answers starting coming to me in a variety of ways like the radio, billboards, signs, books and other assorted ways. If receiving answers isn't happening to you, then you might want to ask more questions or try to remember the questions that you are asking.

THE LORD'S PRAYER

The Lord's Prayer is a common Christian prayer. It sums up our relationship to GOD and our fellow man. This is the prayer Jesus taught his disciples:

Our Father, which art in heaven,
Hallowed be Thy Name.
Thy Kingdom come.
Thy will be done on earth,
As it is in heaven.
Give us this day our daily bread.
And forgive us our trespasses,

As we forgive those that trespass against us.
And lead us not into temptation,
But deliver us from evil.
For Thine is the kingdom,
The power, and the glory,
For ever and ever.
Amen.

"Our Father" means that we have the same Father and that we are His children. We are all brothers and sisters. We are offspring of the Creator. God lives in Heaven. That heaven can and should be created on earth. We need His nourishment one day at a time to enable us to forgive our brothers and sisters, the same way that we need forgiving. We need His help when confronted by The Enemy. He has the power that we need. The power is available to all who ask for it and work towards applying it, One Shot at a Time.

HELL AND HEAVEN

I don't know if Hell is a real place or not. Who am I to say that Hell is or is not a real place that we go when we die if we deserve it. But that concept doesn't work for me. What I certainly can get my head wrapped around is my own personal suffering. I have been in Hell on earth. I have experienced it. I was burnt from my anger at life, God and others. To me it is a state of mind but is most certainly real. The concept of eternal burning in literal Hell is a concept that doesn't work for me. I do believe in Hell on earth.

Conversely, I have no idea if literal Heaven exists. Again, who am I to say it does or does not exist? Will I upon my death be sent up into the clouds to join my Creator, my father, pet dogs and other fallen friends? I most certainly would like to believe this. I just don't know. But what I do know is that I have experienced Heaven (or at least a version of it) right here on earth. I have experienced what Moses was calling the Promised Land; what Buddha was calling Nirvana; and what Jesus called Heaven. I have experienced the here and NOW like Eckhard Tolle refers to in The Power of Now and A New Earth.

75

Abe Lincoln said "Show me a church that believes in only the Golden Rule, 'Do unto others as you would have them do unto you.' I would join that church, but I don't belong to one because I can't find one."

I belong to a Christian Church. I have many friends there. All of them try to practice the Golden Rule. The youth group for my two daughters has been invaluable. My daughters go on two mission trips annually. I have served on the beach mission trip for the past 3 years. It is a magical experience, and I get more out of it then the kids I am serving or the underprivileged kids they are serving. It is a great joy. This church does a lot for others. It works for me. When I was a child, my family took me to church. I didn't have a choice. I was confirmed in a Christian Lutheran Church. When mandatory confirmation was over I was given a choice about continuing with my participation. I chose to not participate. I walked away.

I spent 15 years in the wilderness. I suffered during those lost years. I realize now that I was the one who walked away. The God of My Understanding didn't go anywhere. I was the one who got blocked off from God and others by my selfishness, fears, angers, sadness, guilt, closed-mindedness and pride. I wanted out of this Hell. I didn't want to suffer anymore. However, my mind was slammed shut on the God idea.

Maybe it was the Hell concept of burning for all eternity that I was struggling with. Maybe it was the stories that simply couldn't be true because they defied any type of logic. Maybe it was the money portion of church. I wasn't alone. Many others had turned their back on religion for many legitimate reasons such as the same sex marriage issue, perceived holier-than-thou attitudes, judgmental statements, or unbelievable Bible stories like Jonah being swallowed by a whale and Noah's ark. Also, people have been personally hurt by others in the church and haven't gone back. I was one of these people. I turned my back on God by turning my back on church and religion. Regardless of why, my mind was closed, and it needed to be opened. My way worked some of the time. Freedom, peace, and joy were desired but the results were inconsistent at best. Joy was temporary. I certainly wasn't free or at peace the majority of the time.

Here is where the Spirit of the Universe came to my rescue through a book called Sermon on the Mount by Emmitt Foxx. Foxx posed a simple question to his readers. It doesn't matter how we view Jesus. Whether he was God or the only Son of God or just another human being who found a way out of suffering. A human being? HMMM, I pondered. This was a new thought. What really mattered he said was "This guy was arguably one of the most popular figures in human history. So doesn't it beg the question of why?" Isn't the only thing that really matters what this guy is trying to tell us? It was through this concept that I was able to lay aside my prejudice against religion and open my mind enough for the Spirit's seeds of miracles to form.

I had my first spiritual awakening when I suddenly realized for the first time that I was totally free from my mental obsession for drinking. It was a miracle! It was a miracle that this obsession disappeared and was totally removed. I was free!

About 6 months later, I was pondering the question of "What happened to me?" Wow, this is great because I was really changed! I was free, had peace and was joyful. I asked "How do my kids get this?" "How do others get this?" Surely they don't have to suffer like I did to get this amazing feeling. God had done for me what I couldn't do for myself. But how? Who and what was this God of My Understanding? I didn't understand this God of My Understanding. Was it a him, a her, or an it? I had questions. Lots of questions.

Two days later I saw it! While in a church worship service with my wife and two girls with the band playing and words on the screen. "This little light of mine, I'm gonna let it shine. Hide it under a bushel NO." It was the season of Epiphany, and I was having an epiphany. The answers to my questions had been right in front of me the entire time. My entire life I was blind, but now I see. I was lost, and now I was found. I was in tears. I felt like I had come home. I felt a profound peace, a knowing that I belonged. I understood that it had been under my nose the entire time. I had a sense of hope that my kids could experience what I had found without having to nearly destroy themselves in the process.

"I was lost, but now am found" – "Amazing Grace" John Newton

I didn't know what I didn't know about spirituality. It was only because of my suffering that I needed to seek God again. It wasn't until I started seeking that I found it. My story is one of amazing grace, and I found it in spirituality. After I woke up spiritually, I was healed mentally. I was able to embrace religion again for my wife and two daughters. I did it for them. I am so glad I did, or I would have short changed my life and my family's life. We are much better off as a direct result.

The good news is I found The Promised Land. However, I had to go through Hell first. I couldn't find the solution until I understood the problem. The problem was The Enemy within me, Invisible Landmines and my lack of Landmine Navigation skills. I had to have enough willingness, honesty, and open mindedness in order to seek the solution that would free me from my self-constructed prison. I also had to have enough hope in order to continue on the journey of seeking.

"Carry on my wayward son. There will be peace when you are done. Lay your weary head to rest. Don't you cry no more." – "Carry on My Wayward Son" Kansas

THE KINGDOM OF GOD IS NEAR

Jesus said the Good News is that the Kingdom of God is near. It was so near to us that it was actually inside of us, all of us. It was all around us. All the time. But I didn't know this. I was unaware. It was only because my circumstances went beyond my control that I became willing to seek a way out of Hell. To my surprise and amazement. I found Heaven. I found Heaven right here on earth.

Moses called it the Promised Land. Jesus called the solution Heaven. Buddha called it Nirvana. Many commonly refer to it as light. Some call it Paradise. Call it anything you want. The only thing that matters is that you desire it and are willing to seek it. It is in the seeking that one finds it.

Jesus brought his listeners the Good News that the Kingdom of God was near, that you could actually see God, and that you could experience Heaven on earth. He was saying that all things were possible with God's help. He was talking about freedom from suffering. He was talking about healing the blind and healing the sick. But he said that there was a requirement, "You must be reborn, if you want to experience the kingdom." John 3:3

How about Buddha? He talked about Nirvana and becoming enlightened through the four noble truths. Moses was talking about the

Promised Land. He was liberating his people from bondage. The church says we are in bondage to sin and can't free ourselves. I believe that all of these historical figures were spiritual masters. Meaning they had mastered their craft. Their craft was showing the PATHWAY out of suffering and into a state of freedom, peace, and joy.

THE PRODIGAL SON

We are like the prodigal son in the story in the Christian Bible. (Luke 15: 11-32) I never understood it, and probably never cared to understand it until I read it after my spiritual awakening. Then I got it. I was like the prodigal son who had everything, but left his home to live on his early inheritance. He went out into the world and squandered his fortune. He was down and out and realized he was in worse shape than his father's farm employees. He realized he needed to return home and ask his father to take him in again but as a farm hand.

His father rejoiced and threw a party. His father knew his son had learned life's lesson of gratitude through the pain that God allows. A prodigal boy had left home, but had returned a different man. He had grown through pain and was ready to move forward with life in a successful manner. The point is this is my story. It is the story of a lot of us that fell prey to the misery of The Enemy's lies and needed to recover our freedom, peace and joy.

GENTLEMAN

We strive to be gentle. My grandfather was a gentleman. He was calm, wise, funny, responsible, and gentle. Perhaps he was born that way. Perhaps he had so much suffering that he had to find a solution to peace. I am not sure. What I am sure of is that I am grateful to have known him and played many, many rounds of golf with him. I fished with him and lived with him for a period of time. I watched how he lived, respected his actions, and wanted to be like him. He was a great example of a gentle man, a gentleman. This is how we strive to conduct ourselves after we have recovered.

We are moving forward with our lives. We have built our house on a rock. We have built it on a reliance on God. All things are temporary, but God's love is eternal. Building our life around God's love is reliable. It works, just like building a house on a rock or like the castles in Game of Thrones. If something is built on sand, it can fall down easier. If I build my life on temporary material things, it has a better chance of falling.

3 AM

I was making a sales call on a business in the southern mountains of Virginia. This middle aged female owner had a compound. She worked and lived there. Her house sat on this large pond or little lake. She had one daughter's house next to hers on the left and another daughter's house on the right. There was room for more houses to go up for future grandchildren, etc. She obviously made a lot of money. She was gracious enough to see me when I stopped by unannounced which was my standard M.O. She allowed me 5 minutes to introduce myself and my company. She heard what we might do for her business. Then she started telling me her story. She started telling me how she had suffered, and the business was nothing. She had nothing. She then said she had turned to GOD and had offered herself to Him. She started living for God. She got happy. She found Heaven. She now has this prosperous business employing others in the small town, and money follows. She then stated that it confused her that God wanted to talk to her at precisely 3 AM. Not 2:55 or 3:05. Exactly 3. I didn't think much about this until I started waking up around 3 am. I really tried to listen. I heard nothing. I never received a message. It was quite frustrating. I asked, "If you are going to wake me up, then tell me what you want." But I don't think I said it so calmly and politely. This repeated a few more times. Then I decided that I was not getting up to listen to the Big Guy the next time unless it was exactly 3:00 on the nose. That night I woke up and looked at the clock and what time was it? 3:00 exactly. I started listening. I grabbed a pen and notepad of paper. I started writing. It seemed like the pen was moving on its own. I scribbled out about 8 pages of stuff. Some of which are in this book. Some were boulders in my backpack that needed to be discarded. But all items had to do with eliminating The Enemy and living in peace.

WHAT WAS THE BIG GUY THINKING?

What the hell is this strange place where we live really all about? I have been seeking the answer to this question all my life. This collection of writings probably won't make any sense to the person who hasn't pondered the ultimate question, "What the hell is this life all about?" Well, my friends, it appears that we are here to experience it. Life is meant to be enjoyed. It also appears it was meant to be a place to learn lessons. Some say project Earth is a unique place called Urantia. That once we have learned our lessons here then we can advance to other places to pass on the wisdom. Will we pass wisdom on to other worlds or to other lives? Who knows? However, it does appear that most people (and me for sure) have to learn by failing. Failing is painful. Therefore, if this place is about learning, then it will be a painful experience. When and if I get to question the Big Guy, I will start with "Why do dogs live such short lives?"

WRESTLING WITH THE BIG GUY

I have spent many hours yelling, arguing, and questioning God. Why is life like this? Why is there so much pain and suffering in the world? A German pilot intentionally flew a plane into the Alps recently and killed 150 people on board. A random shooter can massacre dozens of kids at a school. I don't want these things to happen. But I don't have any control over it, and therefore, Acceptance is my answer. Do I want to be free, have peace, and experience joy? If so, then questioning God isn't going to get me there. Playing God doesn't work. Therefore, it is a choice. My choice. Always, my choice is to focus on the good in the world or the bad. However, when I die and rejoin my Creator, I do have some questions for Him, Her or It. In the end, WE are NOT God. We can't control what God does or doesn't do. Therefore, we simply need to accept life on life's term. We need to turn our focus to what we can control and that is our attitude and actions

CHAPTER 12

MY STORY

My parents were wonderful but young. They were both 21 when I was born. They divorced when I was 2 and again at 10. Yes, they were married and divorced from each other twice. I was an only child. I don't blame either one of them for my depression or alcoholism. I had a good childhood. It became a lifetime goal of mine to never get divorced so my children could experience a together family unit.

As an only child, I kept myself occupied with my imagination, sports, and friends. I always had the ball of the season: football, basketball, baseball, and golf. Of course, lake ice hockey, boating, and swimming went along for the ride. Michigan is a wonderful place in the summer time. It was golf that played an important role in my story. I was so fortunate to have a golf club put in my hands by my grandmother when I was 8. I had a large backyard to build my own little course that I wore out before and after school. I played 3 balls around it at a time. I imagined that each ball was a different tour player: Tom Watson, Arnold Palmer, Jack Nicklaus, Gary Player, Lee Trevino and a host of others. I kept stats and had an organized tour. Like I said, I never had a problem being bored; I was always doing and creating.

It was 1982, and I was 12. I came home from school, and my mother with whom I was living most of the time told me we were going to my grandparent's house in Ohio. This seemed odd. A spontaneous trip? Midweek? My hunch was right. We were heading to my grandmother's funeral, my dad's mom. The woman who put my first golf club in my hand and with whom I played countless rounds of golf had killed herself.

I didn't understand her suicide. Rarely do people understand it, let alone a young kid who worshipped her. She had a long time problem with depression and alcoholism. It ended. Unfortunately, she went down in family history that way. Selfish and crazy. I don't blame this event for my depression or alcoholism, but the medical community has proven both conditions are diseases which tend to run through families based on heredity.

It was about this time that I was confirmed in the Lutheran church and given the choice of continuing on with church or not. I chose not. I wasn't rebelling, but I wasn't buying it either. I was simply avoiding the subject. I didn't need it. Over the next few years, I continued to play a lot of golf with my Dad and his Dad. I was so fortunate to have played over 100 rounds of golf with them. Many rounds were walking and talking. I had my first big decision to make as an incoming HS freshman. I could play and start on the varsity golf team or continue my love of football. Both sports were in the fall. I struggled with this decision which was a recurring theme going forward. I chose golf. It seemed logical as it was possible to make a career out of golf vs football. Alhough, I loved football more. I ended up starting and being the MVP my freshman season. It was a good long term decision!

Entering my sophomore golf season, I remember being somewhat discontent. I wanted to be popular in school, and I always felt insecure. I always felt inferior for some reason. I later learned that it is my disease. I don't believe it was because my father had remarried and had another kid. It wasn't because my Mom had remarried, and my stepfather was living with me. It was simply because I was a kid that was unaware of the problem and the solution.

I found a temporary solution that year. It was alcohol. OMG, it made me feel popular. It made me confident. It made all my problems disappear for a while. I thought I had found my solution to life.

From this point on, I was either drinking, hungover from drinking, or thinking about my next drink. My priorities of grades, being a good son, and golf had been replaced with partying, skirt chasing, and hanging with friends. Needless to say that Big Ten scholarship didn't happen.

My mom's new husband got cancer and died. My dad's new marriage failed. I went to live with him for a while and drank more. I was kicked off the golf team for drinking during my junior year. I was busted again, and kicked off the team indefinitely. The sport I loved was gone, but I really didn't care. I was living to party at this point. I was obsessed. I was a prisoner to The Enemy and its ways. I didn't have a solution until I was caught buying beer illegally at age 16 and sentenced to probation and my first AA meeting.

This was my wakeup call! I was now aware of the problem or that there might be a problem. I did what was asked of me over the next 3 months, learned a lot, and was reinstated on the golf team for my senior year. What I learned most of all was that I needed to be more careful with my drinking (my solution to life) because authority figures could take my solution away from me.

I stayed out of trouble for the most part and attended Ferris State University in Big Rapids, Michigan. Ferris had the first Professional Golf Management program in the country, was close by, and had affordable state tuition. It was designed for the person who wanted to be club pro. Perfect for me. It had a Marketing degree with a PGM Minor. These were great years. Happy years. Drinking years.

I went on an internship to Phoenix, TPC Scottsdale. It was a pretty cool experience for a 19 year old Michigan kid. My next internship I separated from the crowd of friends in order to focus on not drinking and growing up. Of course, this concept was a joke. The party scene was everywhere, and I was in the middle of it. My internship was at the Lake of Ozarks in Missouri at Tan Tara Resort. It was there that I met my future wife.

We met while working at the golf course one day. She opened the restaurant side as an intern from Michigan State University. We both were: 21, Geminis, Michiganders, blonde, Lutheran and both only children of educators. The stars had aligned. And of course, she liked to party. So, we did. It was a great summer. At the end of the summer, she went to study in London for a term while I continued on my internship. We wrote letters, and I picked her up at the airport upon arrival. We were together.

My best friend from HS, Brian, came up to live with me at FSU for Spring Term 1991. He was a bright star, everyone loved him. We had played #1 and #2 on the HS golf team. He planned to go to FSU after HS but chose MSU instead for a semester than came home to start a kitchen design career which he was good at, of course. He was good at everything. At the end of the semester, Brian and his dad were going to go fishing with my dad and me up to our cabin in Kipawa, Quebec, Canada. This was an incredible place. It was a two day drive including pulling a boat 6 hours north of Toronto. Then we would put the boat in the water and ride another 25 miles into Echo Bay Camp. I was so excited about this trip because I had never had this trip with just my dad and me. I also knew that soon I was going south to chase a golf ball, and I wasn't sure if the Kipawa trip would ever happen again. Plus, my dad had other children and other commitments. Brian and his dad backed out at the last minute, but my dad and I were headed on our trip of a lifetime as I saw it. You see, I was fortunate to have gone up to this cabin for 2 or more weeks every summer to fish for walleye and Northern Pike. Walleye are the best tasting fish in the whole world, and Pike are a monster fight to reel in.

We arrived at Kipawa and were met by the proprietor of the camp, Wolf Foubert, a French American Indian. He handed my Dad a note. It said, "Brian drowned. Call Jane." It was devastating.

Jane was the mom of my other best friend, Bob. She half way raised me as I was always at her house growing up. I couldn't believe it. How did this happen? This couldn't have happened. Brian and my other college roommates evidently thought it was a good idea to try to swim across the river at night after celebrating the end of the term. My roommates made it. Brian did not.

We turned around immediately to return. I gave a eulogy and will never forget looking over to his parents and sister with my deepest sadness and guilt. I carried this guilt for the next 10 years. If Brian wouldn't have listened to me to come up to Ferris and join me, then this wouldn't have happened. If I wouldn't have gone on the fishing trip and was there with him, surely this wouldn't have happened. I was beyond angry. I was angry at God for allowing this to happen. I was angry for my dream trip with my dad to have been cancelled. It was here that I made a decision to part with God. If there was a God, then He was NOT loving. I am out.

Upon graduation, my future wife and I took off for Orlando, Florida. It was my last internship and first job with Marriott Golf at the World

Center. She was along for the ride. We got engaged. There was trouble in paradise though. I was drinking a lot and was discontent. She wrote me a letter that I kept for years. It basically said, you are great but your behaviors related to drinking are not. She was having her doubts and rightfully so.

My internship was over, and my college buddy suggested I come up and interview with him at Charlotte Country Club. I did. We called the wedding off, and I moved up to Charlotte. However, she decided to follow me, and we got married. We bought a house. We enjoyed being a young married couple. However, my drinking and discontent continued.

Charlotte CC was a great club. It was a tremendous opportunity for a young pro to learn and put in his time before getting his own head pro gig. But she was a Monday thru Friday working girl. Being a pro at CCC required me to be at the club Tuesday through Sunday. Mondays were the only day off, and I played golf and partied with my other pro buddies that day. Life had put me in a crossroads. I couldn't see continuing on this way. I was never seeing my new young wife and breaking my promise to myself of never getting divorced like my parents did. Nor could I see giving up the only career I ever wanted, a club pro. This conflict led to more drinking and more unhappiness. Looking back now, I sure wish I hadn't gone it alone. I wish that I hadn't tried to handle my life and its decisions on my own. I wish I had been aware of the Solution, and I most certainly wish I would have acted on it. Sadly, I didn't take Action, and my career as a private club pro ended.

In the spirit of pursuing happiness and having a win-win between family and career, I started my own golf school. This helped out the situation because I could take Sundays off. It was the best of both worlds. However, after 2 years, I was getting restless, irritable and discontent. I was teaching until 9 pm most nights and all I could think about at 5 pm on was a cold Budweiser. I would come home with beer on my breath and an open 12 pack. There was always boxed wine in the fridge, so she couldn't tell how much I was drinking. There was always Tanquery Gin in the cabinet. My best friend and solution to life was always close and was working for me, or so I thought. What a lie that was.

The golf school was successful but I didn't think it was successful enough to continue doing for the rest of my life. So I let it go and took a sales job. I ended up selling office copiers for 2 years before getting into the Operating Room in medical sales, which was the goal. The chase for money was on. If I couldn't be a club pro then I thought I would be a member of the country club. Our first child Paige came along at this point in 1999. What a joy! I was a dad. Surely this would get me sober and responsible, right? Wrong.

The dot com boom was on, and I was lured away from my new medical sales career to join a college buddy for a golf software startup with all the hopes of a homerun .com startup. Of course it went bust, as did most in 2001, except for Amazon.

The .com job ended, I felt like I was cursed. My wife had had enough. It was one thing to be drinking all the time, and it was another to be unhappy. It was yet another to be unemployed, miserable, and drunk. She gave me the ultimatum, "Stop drinking, or Paige and I are gone." Can you blame her?

The problem with this is I knew I drank too much. I was aware of this. I also was aware that my way wasn't working anymore. I was aware that alcoholics kill themselves like my selfish and crazy grandmother. But I was going it alone. I was dealing with The Enemy all by myself. I was unaware of the solution of Embracing the WE.

We went into marital counseling. What a shocker it was to hear that my drinking was the red flag in our relationship. What I wanted above all else was to be a great Dad, stay married, and yet drink some of the time. Somehow, we all agreed to a drinking contract. I convinced them and myself that it would be ok if I only had 3 drinks anytime I wanted and once a month I was allowed to blow it out. Well 9 days into this agreement, my wife was out of town, and I blew it out. All by myself, while I was watching our one year old Paige. I woke up the next morning to sheer terror. The gig was up. I hadn't even considered the contract. All I cared about was getting shit faced. I knew I had a problem. The denial of reality was so strong. It was simply too powerful to overcome alone. At least it was for me. I was on the unemployment line. I was facing an angry wife who wanted me out. The reality was my life's solution of drinking was not working anymore. It was dark. Really dark. It was darkest before the dawn.

It was time to stop going it alone and Embrace the WE. It was time to ask others for help. It was time to ask God for help. But how could I? God wasn't even real. Or if he was, he surely didn't care about me. How could he? He allowed both my besty and my golf mentor to die. How could I embrace this invisible power? The answer was because I had to. I was backed into a corner. The suffering finally made me willing.

I had been suffering for years. I had been causing pain for my loved ones for years. My way was not working. However, it was now time to face the music and accept the fact that my way wasn't working. My way of going it alone was not working anymore. I had to do something different. I chose to Embrace the We. And thank God I did.

I had to start with Embracing the Horizontal WE. I had to start listening and doing what others told me to do. Others had experience staying sober. Others had experience being free, at peace, and joyful. I wanted this. I needed this.

I was sober for about a month, but I still was not ready to Embrace the Vertical WE when I asked an experienced new friend of mine about God, the God of His Understanding. He said: You don't have to believe in God or a Higher Power. All you have to do is be willing to believe. I said, "What If I am not willing to believe?" He said, "Are you willing to believe that I believe?" I said, "Hell, yes, I can believe that," I said. And so it began. My willingness to Embrace the Vertical WE grew one day at a time. Day by day I was moving towards the light and away from the darkness. I was 6 months sober, and it suddenly dawned on me that God had done for me what I couldn't do for myself. God had removed my drinking mental obsession. This was the first piece of evidence that this Vertical We was real. That He was helpful, friendly, and cared about me. It was shortly after this discovery that I started to sincerely seek an understanding of Him.

I started seeking understanding of this God that I didn't understand. I started to seek the elusive vertical WE. I wanted to know what had happened to me! I was free, at peace and had joy! I wanted more of the good stuff. I was pursuing happiness. I was willing to seek with an open mind. It is in the seeking that one finds. It is in finding the truth that sets us free.

I started asking questions of myself, only to myself. What happened blew my mind. I started getting answers to my questions from sources that didn't know I had asked the questions. How could this be? The answers came from other people delivering answers without me asking them. The answers came in songs. The answers came in books, billboards, signs, and church. Yes, church. The answers had been right in front of me the entire time but I had been blind. I was lost, and now I was found. I was blind and now I see. Amazing Grace!

Life was good. I was still married and developing enough trust with my wife that a 2nd girl came along, Abby. I was back working as a sales rep in the golf industry. I was sober, happy, and enjoying the benefits of my new found relationship with God. It worked.

Life was continuing to be fantastic for another 10 years. Sure there were disappointments, like my father tragically dying at 57 in 2005. There were lost jobs through no fault of my own. There were marital disagreements, teenage/child issues, and health issues. But overall life was good. I was sober, but my life was slowly taking a downturn that I wasn't aware of. I was growing depressed. I was believing Enemy lies again. I was growing discontent with my wonderful life.

I had started a company selling software to the golf industry, a field I had been in for 10 years. It didn't work out. Again, with no fault of my own. I blamed God. Here we go again. A God that wants to punish me. A God that doesn't have my back. It grew dark again.

Feb 6, 2016, my wife said she wanted out. We had been together for 26 years. I tried to convince her that this was a bad idea, but I couldn't. She moved out May 20th of that same year.

I was very fortunate to have evidence that the God of My Understanding was real, and that it could save me from the darkness if I Embraced the WE. I sought God with all my heart that same way I had years before. I came to him like a desperate little child.

I was very fortunate to have developed skills in navigating (life's) Landmines. I sought out advice from my friends with experience. They all told me blue skies were on the horizon. That this too would pass. That this would all be ok, and I would once again have freedom from The Enemy's darkness. I would know peace and have joy. They were right, but I had to work for it. I communicated daily with my Mom, friends, advisors, and God. All throughout the day I surrendered the results of my new life One Shot at a Time. It was these people that God worked through to help me. It is through them that I experienced God. My new testimony is that I asked for peace, strength, and guidance each morning and received it. I still do.

Looking back, I can now see things more clearly. I was depressed. The Enemy was winning. I didn't have enough Awareness, Willingness, and Self-honesty. I wasn't willing to apply and practice the skills I had. I had become complacent in my daily practice. I was going it alone and wasn't Embracing the WE as much as I could have. I wish I would have had the Awareness and Willingness back when I was 16 that I do now. I wish I would have been aware of my depression. I wonder what might have been. But that is a fool's errand, a breach of One Shot at a Time, and not a healthy choice to ponder long.

Today, I am choosing to be happy. I am free, at peace and have an opportunity to experience joy. Out of the darkness comes the light. It is always darkest before the dawn. I have my own company called Custom Coaching Solutions. We focus on life and recovery coaching for male teenagers and adults suffering with substance abuse and depression. I am trying to help my clients develop skills to deal with The Enemy, to navigate Landmines, and to spiritually transform into their highest and best potential. I am trying to serve others with my personal experience which gives me joy. I am grateful for my life. I am grateful for my family and friends. I am grateful for what I have. I am trying to do my best to take life One Shot at a Time and enjoy the journey called Life.

Printed in the United States
By Bookmasters